EGYPTIAN
FLAVORS

Dyna Eldaief

EGYPTIAN FLAVORS

50 RECIPES

The American University in Cairo Press
Cairo   New York

First published in 2021 by
The American University in Cairo Press
113 Sharia Kasr el Aini, Cairo, Egypt
One Rockefeller Plaza, New York, NY 10020
www.aucpress.com

Dar el Kutub No. 26172/18
ISBN 978 977 416 927 4

Dar el Kutub Cataloging-in-Publication Data

Eldaief, Dyna
        Egyptian Flavors: 50 Recipes / Dyna Eldaief.—Cairo: The American
University in Cairo Press, 2021.
        p.   cm.
        ISBN 978 977 416 927 4
        1.   Food—Egypt
        2.   Cooking, Egyptian
        3.   Cooking—Egypt
        641.50962

1 2 3 4 5   25 24 23 22 21

Design concept by **studio medlikova**
Design and layout by Sally Boylan

Printed in China

CONTENTS

INTRODUCTION

Egypt has a rich history with many significant developments going back to ancient Egypt. Not only was this ancient civilization pioneering in architecture, astronomy, medicine, and the creation of a writing system, but it was a culture rich in design, music, art, and cuisine. The life line for the country has always been the Nile River where ancient civilization took root and blossomed, using successful farming practices developed around this remarkable water source. Tomb paintings depict animals and crops as food sources, and dishes from ancient Egypt have been passed down through the generations, retaining time-honored characteristics. *Molokhiya* was depicted as a food for the pharaohs and can still be found today across the globe. In my homeland of Australia, I buy it in various markets in the city, although I can only find it fresh for a short period in the summer months. The rest of the year I buy it frozen. My father still grows a crop of this herb every year and we are all invited to celebrate the first pick of the season—and often the last as well. My children have grown up loving this dish and it is almost always their first choice for a birthday dinner. It is amazing to think that we are still eating some of the same dishes that Egyptians ate thousands of years ago.

For this book I have put together a collection of fifty traditional Egyptian recipes to give you an insight into the history of Egyptian cuisine and its indigenous ingredients, as well as offering nutritional information and something a little more personal—what the dish signifies to me. It is my hope that you will enjoy this book, not only for its recipes and the history that goes with them, but also that it might inspire you to use these incredible ingredients in dishes of your own. For me, cooking food that is part of my heritage is like looking through a portal to the past and I invite you to come on the journey with me.

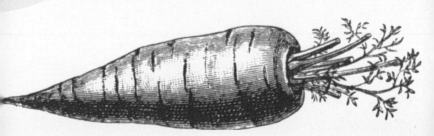

DIPS, STARTERS, AND SOUPS

'EISH MIHAMMAS | PITA CHIPS

Serves: 6–8

These intensely crunchy and immensely satisfying pita chips have become hugely popular in the West over the last few years, finding their way into many supermarkets and delicatessen stores. In the Middle East however, they have been enjoyed for far longer than that. They are often served as an appetizer at wedding receptions where it can be hard to stop eating them before the next course is served! While pita bread can be simply dried in the oven or on the grill as it is when making *fatta* (bread and rice soaked in stock), for me this is the equivalent of wearing pyjamas to a wedding! In the same way that one should dress up properly for a wedding, it is worth making the effort with this dressed-up version of pita bread too.

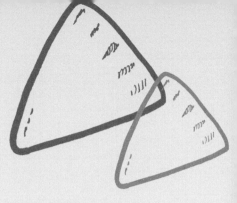

Ingredients:

5 pieces (1 packet) white or whole wheat pita bread

Vegetable oil, for frying

Sea salt flakes

Dukkah, to serve (optional, page 12)

• Cut each pita bread into quarters, and then cut each quarter in half, making 8 triangles.

• Heat the oil in a medium-sized pan. The oil is hot enough for frying when it can brown a small piece of bread in 10–15 seconds. Gently place 2 or 3 pieces of bread at a time into the oil and fry until just golden in color, before turning over to cook the other side.

• When both sides are lightly colored, remove and place on a paper towel. Lightly sprinkle with salt flakes, or *dukkah* (page 12), and serve alongside dips such as *hummus bi-t-tahina* (page 16) or *baba ghanoug* (page 18).

DUKKAH | ALMOND SPICE BLEND

Makes: 2 cups

Dukkah is a blend of spices and nuts which are usually toasted and then combined in a pestle and mortar. The word *dukkah* derives from an Arabic word which means 'to crush' or 'to pound.' Nuts such as peanuts, almonds, or hazelnuts can be used along with cumin, coriander, sesame seeds, salt, and sometimes even dried herbs, and can vary in their composition and quantity.

Traditionally the blend is served with good quality olive oil and fresh bread. Alternatively, it is delicious sprinkled on top of my crispy pita chips (page 10) before serving. Be careful not to overcook the sesame seeds when dry toasting as they will become bitter if they brown.

Ingredients:

60 g (2 oz) / ½ cup sesame seeds
30 g (1 oz) / ½ cup coriander seeds
1 tablespoon cumin seeds
1 teaspoon whole peppercorns
1 teaspoon salt
140 g (5 oz) / 1 cup unsalted almonds, roasted

• Heat a frying pan without oil and add sesame seeds, coriander seeds, cumin seeds, and whole peppercorns. When the spices become fragrant, remove from the heat and leave to cool.

• Place the spices in a spice blender or food processor, along with the salt and almonds, and pulse to a coarse powder. Even better, pound the ingredients using a pestle and mortar so the oils are released—this will give your *dukkah* more texture and character.

• Serve sprinkled over crunchy pita chips (page 10) or place in a bowl alongside cold-pressed olive oil and fresh bread. Dip pieces of bread into the oil and then into the *dukkah*.

TAHINA | TAHINI DIP

Makes: 150 g (5½ oz)

Tahina is a dip made from a sesame seed paste called tahini. It is widely used throughout the Middle East in *halva*—sweet confections—as well as in savory dips, sauces or spreads, dressings, or even to thicken soups. It has a dense texture high in oil, fibre, and calcium but lower levels of sugar and saturated fats like those found in peanut butter. In Alexandria, unlike other parts of Egypt, it is also added to—or served on top of—*fuul medammis*, Egypt's national dish.

COOK'S TIP

This delicious dip can be served with crudités or as a perfect accompaniment to grilled or fried fish.

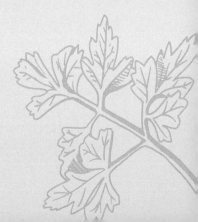

Ingredients:

3 tablespoons tahini paste
¾ teaspoon crushed garlic
¼ teaspoon salt, or to taste
½ teaspoon ground cumin
Juice of half a lemon or 1 tablespoon white vinegar
½ cup (125 ml) water
Small handful of fresh flat-leaf/Italian parsley, chopped

• Place the tahini paste, crushed garlic, salt, cumin, and lemon juice or vinegar in a blender and mix well to form a smooth paste.
• Add water a little at a time and keep mixing well. If the mixture begins to separate, add more water and keep mixing until smooth. If the mixture looks thicker than desired, add a little more water.
• Add the parsley then pulse just enough to combine. Serve immediately or refrigerate in an airtight container. This will keep for a couple of days.

HUMMUS BI-T-TAHINA | HUMMUS DIP

Makes: 450 g (1 lb)

Hummus has become quite well known around the world as a dip. It is one of the easiest and tastiest ways to incorporate chickpeas into your diet. If you are looking to make healthier eating choices, this dip is great as a spread for salad sandwiches and wraps as it is much lower in cholesterol than using butter and has greater nutritional value too.

If you want to prepare the dip in a hurry, you could use a 400 g (14 oz) can of cooked chickpeas instead of the dried ones.

COOK'S TIP

Tahini may be made from hulled or unhulled sesame seeds, and the two versions are different nutritionally, as well as in taste and color. Tahini made with unhulled seeds is richer in vitamins (E, F, and B) and minerals (especially calcium), and it is darker with a stronger flavor. If you decide to use the unhulled version, start with 1 tablespoon of the paste and add more as required, as it is quite difficult to abate the flavor intensity if there is too much to begin with.

Ingredients:

150 g (5½ oz) dried chickpeas
Juice of 1 lemon
2 cloves garlic, crushed
2 tablespoons olive oil
½ teaspoon ground cumin
70 g (2½ oz) tahini paste
Salt, to taste
Ground smoked paprika, to garnish

• Put the dried chickpeas in a bowl, cover with cold water, and leave overnight.
• Drain the chickpeas, place them in a saucepan, and cover with fresh water. Bring to the boil and cook on a high heat for 10 minutes, then reduce the heat and simmer for 2 hours or until soft. Drain.
• Place the chickpeas in a food processor and blend to a smooth consistency. Add the lemon juice, garlic, olive oil, cumin, and tahini and blend until smooth. Taste and season as required.
• Transfer to a bowl, garnish with paprika, and serve or refrigerate. This dip will keep in the fridge for several days and is great as a butter substitute for sandwiches.

BABA GHANOUG | EGGPLANT DIP

Makes: 340 g (12 oz)

This is another tasty dip that incorporates eggplant. This vegetable, with its deep purple–black color and smooth skin, is often underused and understated in cooking. Due to its spongy flesh, it will absorb the flavors of garlic and cumin in this dip beautifully, while also adding texture. Traditionally, the eggplant is roasted whole over an open flame until the skin becomes wrinkly and blackened. Alternatively, it can be roasted in the oven or under the grill. Place it in a closed plastic bag for a few minutes to sweat, then take it out and remove the skin, which will now peel off very easily. The bitterness which can occur in eggplants can be eliminated by squeezing out the liquid before adding it to the dip.

Ingredients:

2 cloves garlic, unpeeled
1 large or 2 small eggplants
7 tablespoons olive oil
½ teaspoon salt, or to taste
4 tablespoons tahini
2 tablespoons chopped parsley, plus extra to garnish
½ teaspoon ground cumin
Juice of 1 lemon

• Heat the oven to 180°C (350 °F/Gas mark 4). Place the garlic on a roasting tray and roast for 15 minutes or until soft. Allow to cool, then remove the flesh from the skin.

• While the garlic is roasting, cook the eggplant. Use a long pair of tongs to hold the eggplant over the medium flame of a gas stove. Keep turning so that the eggplant becomes soft and the skin blackens all over. Remove from the stove and leave to cool slightly, then place into a plastic bag.

• After a few minutes remove the eggplant from the bag and the skin should peel off easily. Put it in a sieve and press gently with a spoon to remove excess liquid.

• Place the eggplant, garlic, olive oil, salt, tahini, parsley, cumin, and lemon juice in an electric blender or food processor and blend. Don't over blend—you're aiming for some texture. Add a little water if the mix is too thick.

• Taste and adjust seasoning if required. Transfer to a bowl and garnish with chopped parsley. Serve with crisp Lebanese flatbread or fresh Turkish bread, or alongside barbecued meat or *kofta*.

SALATIT ZABADI | YOGURT DIP

Makes: 350 g (12½ oz)

In Europe and Australia this dip is known as tzatziki and is available from many supermarkets, but it is such an easy dip to make that you should never need to buy it again—and it tastes delicious when freshly made. The easiest way to make *Salatit zabadi* is by using shop-bought, unsweetened Greek-style yogurt, which is lovely and thick, but if you make your own yogurt it can be thickened and used as well (see Cook's Tip, below).

Traditionally, this dip is served alongside stuffed vine leaves (*mahshi wara' 'enab*, page 62) as a dipping sauce. It adds acidity to the *mahshi* as well as a lovely creaminess.

Ingredients:

1 large Lebanese cucumber, peeled
1 cup (250 g) natural Greek-style yogurt
1–2 cloves garlic, crushed
1–2 teaspoons dried mint, or 1 tablespoon finely chopped fresh mint
Pinch of salt

• Cut the cucumber in half lengthways and remove the seeds from the center. Removing the seeds is not essential, but they carry a lot of water, so keeping the seeds in the dip may make it thin and runny. Pat the cucumber dry using some paper towels, then finely chop or grate the flesh.

• In a bowl, combine the cucumber, yogurt, garlic, mint, and a pinch of salt, then gently mix together. Serve immediately or store in the fridge for up to a week.

COOK'S TIP

• To thicken natural plain yogurt, you will need to strain it using a cheese or muslin cloth. Simply place the amount of yogurt required in the center of the cloth and bring the corners of the cloth together.

• Tie using a rubber band and leave the yogurt parcel draining in a sieve over a bowl for 30 minutes to an hour (depending on the quantity) to remove some of the liquid whey.

• If you find that you have thickened the yogurt too much, add a little of the extracted whey, stirring it back in. Do not leave the yogurt draining all day or overnight as you might end up with cheese!

FUUL MEDAMMIS | SLOW-COOKED FAVA BEANS

Serves: 2

Fuul is the Egyptian word for 'broad beans' (also known as fava beans), and *medammis* is a word meaning 'buried,' which refers to the original cooking method of burying a pot of beans and water under hot coals. Today, most people prepare the dish using a slow cooker; in Egypt they often use a special *dammasa* slow cooker, which has a container of hot water above for topping up the beans as they cook. If you don't have one, use a heavy-based pot with a tight-fitting lid.

Canned broad beans or fava beans are perfect to use here as they save so much time and you can still choose if you want to peel the beans or not. I prefer the smoother texture but it is not essential. *Fuul* can be made in advance, cooled, then refrigerated for up to 2 days or frozen for several months. Thaw out in the fridge overnight, then heat and add the remaining ingredients.

> **COOK'S TIP**
>
> For a heartier *fuul medammis* you could add ½ small tomato, ½ small onion, and ½ small Lebanese cucumber, all very finely diced. Some people like to mash a boiled egg and some feta into the beans too. If adding any or all of these, check the flavor and add more garlic, oil, lemon juice, cumin, or salt as required.

Ingredients:

160 g (5½ oz) dried broad beans
2 tablespoons extra virgin olive oil
1 clove garlic, crushed
1 teaspoon ground cumin
Juice of 1 lemon
Sea salt flakes
Pinch of freshly ground black pepper

• If using dried beans, leave to soak in water overnight, then drain and place in a large saucepan with plenty of fresh water. Bring to the boil, then simmer until tender. This may take 5–6 hours.

• Allow to cool slightly, then remove the skins by squeezing out the flesh of each bean using your thumb and forefinger. Discard the skins and mash the flesh. If you don't want to go to the trouble of peeling the beans, you can purée them with their skins on until you achieve a smooth consistency.

• Add the oil, garlic, cumin, and lemon juice and combine well. Season with salt and pepper and taste to check the balance of flavors, adjusting if necessary.

'EGGAH |
PARSLEY AND ONION OMELET

Serves: 1

Typically eaten at breakfast, this dish is similar to a Western omelet. The parsley gives it a dominant fresh flavor that is wonderful first thing in the morning, and helps to balance the more robust egg and fried onion. This is a great dish to keep in mind for a very quick and easy midweek lunch or dinner. It could also be served sliced as part of a mezze platter, especially if there are vegetarians amongst you.

I love using marinated feta cheese with eggs and it is perfect with this. You can buy feta cheese already marinated or you can make your own. Simply cube some Danish-style feta cheese (creamier and less crumbly than Greek feta) into a glass jar and add garlic, bay leaves, peppercorns, and fresh thyme, then cover the whole lot in olive oil. Store in the fridge and use within a week.

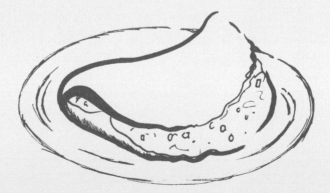

Ingredients:

30 g (1 oz) butter
½ small onion, chopped
Small bunch flat-leaf parsley, finely chopped
2 teaspoons all-purpose flour
2 eggs
Sea salt and freshly ground black pepper
Marinated feta cheese, to serve

• Melt half the butter in a small frying pan over a low heat. Add the onion and fry for 5 minutes until caramelized.
• Add the parsley and flour, and stir for 1–2 minutes. In the meantime, beat the eggs in a bowl and season with salt and pepper. Add the onion and parsley mixture to the eggs and stir well to combine.
• Heat the remaining butter in a frying pan; when it is bubbling, add the egg mixture, spreading it over the pan. Cook until the bottom is golden.
• Fold the omelet in half and serve hot with fresh Lebanese flatbread and feta cheese.

KOSHARI | EGYPTIAN KHICHDI

Serves: 6

Koshari joins *fuul medammis* as one of Egypt's national dishes and is part of the tradition and culinary heritage of this wonderful country. It can be found on the menu in restaurants and as a 'fast food' in shopping center food courts and on street stalls. It is a carbohydrate-loaded meal containing pasta, rice, and lentils, but made really tasty with rich tomato sauce and caramelized onion.

Traditionally the lentils are partially cooked and added to rice to cook further but if you are really short on time you could use canned lentils and chickpeas. The sauce could also be made in advance and kept refrigerated or frozen.

Ingredients:

100 g (3½ oz) brown lentils, washed and drained

1 tablespoon vegetable or rice bran oil

1 onion, diced

60 g (2 oz) or 2 handfuls crushed vermicelli noodles

200 g (7 oz) white long-grain rice

100 g (3½ oz) raw macaroni pasta

120 g (4 oz) boiled or canned chickpeas

Special sauce:

1 tablespoon olive oil
1–2 cloves garlic, crushed
1 teaspoon ground coriander
¼ cup (60 ml) white vinegar
Sea salt and freshly ground black pepper
1 cup (250 ml) water

Rich tomato sauce:

1 tablespoon olive oil
1 medium onion, finely chopped
2 cloves garlic, crushed
1½ cups (375 ml) tomato sauce or passata
¼ teaspoon chili powder (optional)
½ teaspoon ground cumin
¼ teaspoon salt
⅛ teaspoon ground black pepper
1 cup (250 ml) water

Onion garnish:

¼ cup (60 ml) vegetable oil
2 or 3 large onions, sliced

• Begin by making the special sauce. In a small saucepan, heat the oil over a medium heat, then add the garlic and fry for 2 minutes. Add the coriander, vinegar, and a sprinkling of salt and pepper, then add the water and bring to the boil. Remove from the heat and adjust the seasoning as necessary.

• To cook the lentils, put them into a pan with 2 cups (500 ml) of water and bring to a boil. Simmer over a medium heat for 20 minutes then drain.

• In the same pan, heat the oil and fry the chopped onion until soft. Add the vermicelli noodles and cook until just starting to brown. Add the rice and stir for a further 3 minutes, then add 2 cups (500 ml) of fresh water. Bring to the boil then reduce heat to a simmer. Add the drained lentils to the rice. Cover, then simmer for 20 minutes or until the rice is soft and the lentils are cooked through.

• Begin to cook the macaroni at around the same time that you cook the rice. Fill a separate pan with water and a sprinkle of salt and bring to a boil. Add the macaroni to the boiling water and cook until tender, according to packet directions, then drain.

• While the lentils, rice, and macaroni are cooking, prepare the rich tomato sauce. Heat the oil in a pan and fry the onion and garlic until golden brown. Add the tomato sauce or passata, chili powder, cumin, salt, and pepper. Add the water and bring to the boil, then lower the heat and simmer for 20–25 minutes until the sauce has reduced and thickened.

• Prepare the onion garnish. Heat the oil in a saucepan over a medium heat and add the sliced onion. Fry for 20–25 minutes or until the onion is soft and caramelized. Set aside.

• Put the chickpeas in a bowl of boiling water for a few minutes to warm through, then drain. Along with the lentils, rice, macaroni, and sauces, begin to layer the components in a large bowl or oval platter as follows:

1st layer—rice and lentils; 2nd layer—macaroni; 3rd layer—chickpeas; 4th layer—rich tomato sauce; 5th layer—small amount of special sauce; 6th layer—onion garnish.

• Put the rest of the special sauce in a small jug and serve alongside the *koshari*.

TA'MIYA | FALAFEL

Makes: 20+

Falafel is another popular Egyptian dish that is traditionally eaten for breakfast. The patties are made of fried broad (fava) beans that have been soaked overnight, peeled, and blended. In other parts of the Arab world, it is more often made using a mix of fava beans and chickpeas or just chickpeas.

Today, you can buy packaged 'falafel mixes,' in dried and frozen versions, but freshly made falafel tastes far better. Falafel is sometimes served in sandwiches and in pita, and it is often accompanied with *baba ghanoug* (page 18) or *tahina* (page 14). This recipe makes a large quantity but it can easily be frozen and then thawed out before the shaping and frying stages.

Ingredients:
500 g (1 lb) dried broad beans
3 tablespoons coriander seeds
2 onions or 1 bunch spring onions, chopped
2 large cloves garlic, crushed
1 bunch parsley, finely chopped
1 leek, washed thoroughly
2–3 tablespoons ground cumin
2–3 tablespoons ground coriander
1 tablespoon baking powder
Salt and freshly ground black pepper, to taste
2 tablespoons sesame seeds
Rice bran or vegetable oil, for deep-frying

• Soak the beans in water for 24 hours or more to soften them. Drain and skin them by slitting the skin of each one and popping out the flesh. Place in a food processor and blend briefly.

• Roast the coriander seeds by placing them in a small pan and dry-frying them for a few minutes until fragrant. Allow to cool, then crush lightly.

• In the food processor, add the onion, garlic, parsley, leek, cumin, ground coriander, baking powder, and roasted coriander seeds to the broad beans, then add salt and pepper to taste. Blend to a smooth paste in batches, then combine and leave to rest for at least 30 minutes.

• Take a tablespoon of the mixture and shape it into a ball about the size of a walnut shell. Dip into the sesame seeds and place it on a chopping board or large plate and press to flatten it slightly. Repeat until you have used all the mixture. Leave the flattened balls to rest for another 15 minutes.

• Heat some oil in a deep fryer until hot, then fry the falafel in batches until they become a dark, rich, golden-brown color. Remove and drain on paper towels. Serve hot with tahini dip or *baba ghanoug* and fresh bread.

SAMBUSA BI-L-LAHMA | MINCE TRIANGLES

Makes: 21–24

Sambusa is a traditional snack or starter that is eaten through-out the Middle Eastern region, and variations are also found in South and Central Asia, as well as North and South Africa. The recipe is different in each area but can also be unique to each household within a region. It can be made sweet or savory, with meat or with mixed cheeses, or even with a veg-etable mix. This is a meat version made into triangles. The meat filling can easily be made in advance and the triangles assembled on the day of baking. If using filling that has been frozen, make sure it has thawed to room temperature before using. Don't ever be tempted to use hot filling—this will ruin the pastry and make folding it into shape nearly impossible. The parcels can also be made ahead and frozen before baking.

Ingredients:

1 tablespoon olive oil
1 onion, finely chopped
1 teaspoon crushed garlic
300 g (10½ oz) ground beef
1 teaspoon ground coriander
½ teaspoon ground cumin

Salt and freshly ground
  black pepper, to taste
1 cup (250 ml) water
375 g (13 oz) filo pastry
Ghee or melted butter
  for brushing

• Preheat the oven to 180°C (350 °F/Gas mark 4). Heat the oil in a pan, add the onion, garlic, and meat, and fry until browned. Add the spices, salt, and pepper, then pour in the water and allow to simmer, stirring occasionally, until the liquid has evaporated. Remove from the heat and cool.

• Remove all the pastry from the packets and, working quickly, cut the sheets in half. Take one of the top sheets (cover the remaining sheets with a clean damp kitchen towel to keep them from drying out), brush it with melted butter, and fold it in half lengthways.

• Place a tablespoon of the beef mixture on the left-hand corner of the pastry strip, making a triangular shape with the mixture. Fold up the bottom left corner, lifting up the mixture and moving it toward the right, making a triangle shape with the pastry as you cover the filling. Now fold the triangle containing the filling over to the right then down. Continue folding in this manner until all the pastry is used up.

• Repeat the process until you have used all the filling and pastry. Brush the top of each triangle with butter and place on a lightly greased tray, folded side down. Bake for 20–25 minutes until golden brown. Serve immediately.

HAWAWSHI |
CRUNCHY PITA PARCELS

Makes: 4

Hawawshi is one of my favorite dishes. It is a dough filled with spiced ground meat and baked until golden and crispy. In Egypt, the bread is traditionally made fresh, as in the recipe below, and can be found as an appetizer in many restaurants and at social gatherings or eaten as a snack at home. If you don't have much time, you can use pita or Lebanese bread instead. Eliminate what you don't like and add more of what you do to make your very own customized *hawawshi*.

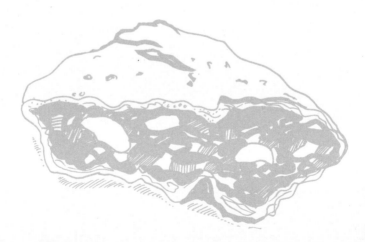

Ingredients:

Filling:

¼ kg (½ lb) ground beef

¼ kg (½ lb) ground lamb

1 onion, finely chopped

1 clove garlic, crushed

2 small tomatoes, seeds removed and finely chopped

¼–½ green capsicum or bell pepper

1 teaspoon salt and freshly ground black pepper, or to taste

1½ tablespoons mixed spice

1 teaspoon allspice or nutmeg

Small handful parsley (optional)

Few drops of hot chilli sauce (optional)

2 tablespoons ghee/clarified butter, melted

Dough:

360 g (12½ oz) plain flour

1½ tablespoons salt

1½ tablespoons sugar

4 teaspoons dry yeast

1½ cups (375 ml) lukewarm water

1 tablespoon vegetable oil or butter

• Preheat the oven to 200°C (400°F/Gas mark 6). First make the filling by combining all the ingredients in a food processor and blend well. Set aside.

• To make the dough, sift the flour and salt into a bowl and make a well in the center. Combine the sugar, yeast, and water in a cup and gently mix together then leave in a warm place for 10 minutes until bubbles form. (If there are no bubbles it means the yeast is dead and you will need to start again with fresh yeast.)

• Add the yeast mixture to the flour and combine. When the dough comes together place it on a floured surface and knead until smooth and elastic. Form into a large ball.

• Drizzle a little oil into a bowl and add the ball of dough, covering it with a clean kitchen towel. Leave to prove for 30 minutes in a warm spot on the kitchen counter or in a warm (not hot) oven.

• Remove the dough from the bowl and knead again before dividing into 8 small balls.

• Taking one ball at a time, press and stretch the dough out on a flat surface with your fingertips until you have 8 discs. Divide the *hawawshi* filling into 4 and place each portion onto one of the discs. Cover with the remaining discs. Press to flatten and fold over the edges to seal, then flatten some more.

• Brush the top with ghee. Perforate the top disc with a fork all over—this will allow steam to escape while cooking. Wrap each *hawawshi* in parchment paper or place them on a well-oiled baking tray.

• Bake for 7–9 minutes or until the parcels are beautifully golden and crispy. Cut and serve.

MOLOKHIYA | MALLOW SOUP

Serves: 4

Molokhiya is a classic Egyptian soup. It is believed to have originated during the time of the pharaohs, as it is depicted in pharaonic tomb paintings, and it is thought that the original name for *molokhiya* is *molokiya*, meaning 'of the kings.' In Egypt this soup is made by chopping the leaves of this herb into very tiny pieces which can be added to the stock fresh or frozen. In Lebanon this soup is made in much the same way although the leaves are left whole when added to the stock.

The chicken used to make the stock can be replaced by 1 rabbit or 500 g (1 lb) topside/round beef, cut into several large portions. Traditionally the meat used to make the stock is served on the side, either plainly boiled or boiled then fried in ghee until golden brown.

The fried garlic and coriander mixture is known as *ta'liya* and it has a few variations. Some cooks add salt, others add onion and/or 1 or 2 teaspoons of tomato paste.

Ingredients:

4 cups (1 liter) chicken stock
400 g (14 oz) frozen *molokhiya* leaves or 750 g (1½ lb) fresh
molokhiya, chopped
3 tablespoons ghee
6 cloves garlic, crushed
1½ tablespoons ground coriander
Salt and freshly ground black pepper, to taste

• Place the stock in a pan and bring to the boil, then reduce the heat and add the chopped *molokhiya*. (If using frozen *molokhiya*, add it to the stock while still frozen.) Leave the pan uncovered and do not stir—just allow the liquid to heat gently until it reaches boiling point, then remove from the heat. Be careful not to overcook *molokhiya* as this can result in separation and a two-layered soup.

• Meanwhile, melt the ghee in a frying pan over a medium heat and add the garlic. Cook until lightly browned, then add the coriander. Stir and remove from the heat.

• Add the garlic mix to the *molokhiya* and stir to combine. If necessary, add some water to achieve the desired consistency and adjust seasoning to taste.

• Serve immediately in bowls with rice or fresh Lebanese or pita bread. The bread can be broken into pieces and then used to scoop up the *molokhiya*, or it can be added to the bowl of soup and eaten with a spoon.

'ADS | SILKY LENTIL SOUP

Serves: 6

This is one of the few soups traditionally eaten during the cooler months in Egypt. It is warm and nutritious, and the flavors of cumin and lemon are wonderful with the lentils. It is easy to find the ingredients in supermarkets and lentils are one of the least expensive sources of protein. They are also a good source of dietary fiber and carbohydrates. This is my go-to soup for anyone who is vegan or has allergies to gluten, nuts, eggs, etc., because it contains none of these and, using only a few ingredients, it is wonderfully simple and tasty. I blend my soup with a stick blender to give it a super smooth consistency.

Ingredients:

1 tablespoon ghee or butter
1 medium onion, chopped
300 g (10½ oz) red lentils
2 teaspoons ground cumin
2 tablespoons lemon juice
½ teaspoon sea salt

• Melt the ghee or butter in a deep pan over a medium heat and add the chopped onion. Fry for 5 minutes or until lightly browned.

• Meanwhile, wash and drain the lentils. When the onion is cooked, remove it to a plate and set aside. Add the lentils to the pot along with 4 cups (1 liter) of water. Bring this to the boil then reduce the heat, cover, and leave to simmer for 30 minutes until cooked, adding more water if the soup is too thick.

• Carefully use a stick blender to blend the soup until smooth. Add the cumin and lemon juice and blend again. Taste before adding salt. Serve with the fried onion on top.

COOK'S TIP

You can use chicken stock rather than water for a richer taste (although obviously not for vegans!). Simply add water to the stock if necessary. This can also be served as a more liquid soup, with fresh Lebanese bread on the side or with small pieces of dried bread broken into the soup. To do this, split the bread into halves, place in a hot oven (200°C/400 °F/ Gas mark 6) for 10–15 minutes, then break into pieces before sprinkling over the soup.

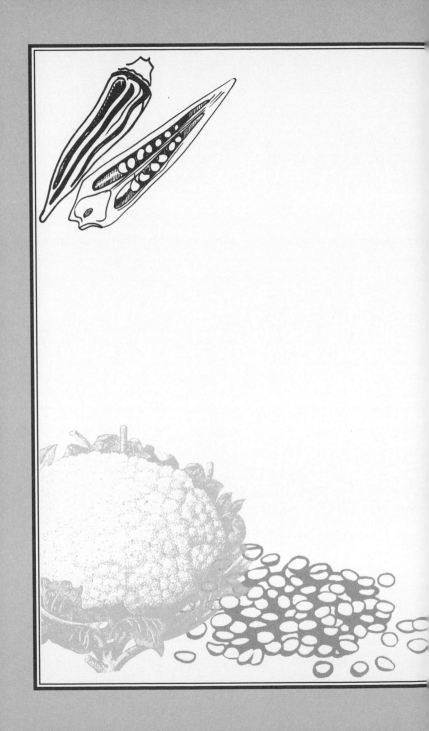

VEGETABLES
AND GRAINS

FATTA | STOCK-SOAKED BREAD WITH RICE

Serves: 4–6

This was one of my dad's signature dishes. I remember him making this more often than mum when I was growing up. Egyptian *fatta* refers to a dish made with 'soaked bread' and is similar to *fatteh* which is Arabic for 'crushed' or 'crumbs.' In Lebanon it is also the basis of the name for *fattoush* salad, which utilizes toasted pieces of pita bread on top of a tangy salad.

In Palestine a similar dish made with chicken is the national dish of Gaza, but versions are made in most of the countries surrounding Egypt including Jordan, Palestine, Lebanon, and Syria. Unlike Egyptian *fatta,* other countries may use yogurt or chickpeas on top but for any version it is a great way to use up stale or dried pita bread.

COOK'S TIP

If making chicken stock at home use chicken drumsticks or thigh pieces. After cooking remove the boiled chicken pieces and serve with the *fatta* in place of the roasted chicken.

Ingredients:

2 loaves Lebanese bread
1½–2 cups (375–500 ml) chicken stock
30 g (1 oz) ghee or butter
4 cloves garlic, crushed
3 tablespoons white vinegar
1 serving of rice with vermicelli (page 76)
2 shallots finely chopped, to garnish (optional)
1 chicken, roasted and cut into pieces

• Preheat the oven to 200°C (400°F/Gas mark 6). Split the bread into halves and place it in the oven for 10–15 minutes until completely dry and golden brown.

• Break the bread into small pieces over a large bowl or stock pot.

• Heat the stock in a pan; bring it briefly to the boil then turn down the heat so that it is simmering gently.

• In a small pan, melt the ghee or butter and fry the garlic until it is just beginning to change color, then add the vinegar and mix well. Take off the heat and add to the stock.

• Pour the garlic and stock mix over the dried broken bread, stir, then add the rice and combine. Place the mixture on a serving plate and arrange the chicken pieces over the top. Garnish with the finely chopped fresh shallots, if using, just before serving.

FASOLYA TABIKH |
ONE-POT BEEF AND BEAN STEW

Serves: 4

The simple heart of this recipe—stewing meat with vegetables and tomatoes—formed the basis of many of the meals I ate at home. My mother was the main cook in our house and dad called her the 'kitchen boss,' but very occasionally my dad was let loose in the kitchen to whip up something for dinner. My siblings and I would refer to his one-pot wonders as 'dads invention number 1, 2, 3, etc.' The funny thing was, dad had no idea what he used from one invention to the next because it was a collection of ALL the vegetables and whatever meat there was in the fridge or freezer. These were dad's versions of *tabikh*, a dish that is cooked like a stew. The dish can be made in a pressure cooker if you have one, which will reduce the cooking time by about half while producing the most tender meat.

COOK'S TIP

You could use cannellini or red kidney beans in place of the black-eyed peas. If you want to increase the vegetable content, add 90 g (3 oz) sweet corn plus 220 g (8 oz) fresh peas or green beans along with the carrots.

Ingredients:

400 g (14 oz) black-eyed peas

1 tablespoon ghee or butter

1 large onion, chopped

500 g (1 lb) beef (shank, topside, or round),
   cut into 10–12 rough chunks

1 teaspoon freshly ground black pepper

1 teaspoon allspice

1 teaspoon mixed spice

2 carrots

140 g (5 oz) thickened tomato paste

1½ cups (375 ml) tomato sauce or passata

• Put the black-eyed peas in a bowl, cover with cold water, and leave to soak overnight. Drain.

• In a heavy-based pan or pressure cooker, melt the ghee or butter over a medium heat and fry the onion until soft and caramelized.

• Add the meat and spices, stir, and allow to cook until the beef chunks are browned.

• While the meat is cooking, peel and dice the carrots. When the meat has browned, add the black-eyed peas and cook for 2 minutes.

• Add the tomato paste and sauce, along with enough water to cover the meat. Cover and cook at a simmer for 50–60 minutes or until the meat is cooked all the way through. Add the carrots and cook for a further 10 minutes. Serve with rice.

ARNABIT FI-L-FORN | BAKED CAULIFLOWER

Serves: 6

There is much more that one can do with cauliflower than just boiling it and serving with a cheese sauce. I love the taste of it when steamed (still with some crunch) and then shallow fried in a little butter. I also like to eat it raw or lightly steamed just as a snack. Traditionally it is cooked with beef but this recipe is a vegetarian version.

Did you know that white cauliflower lacks the chlorophyll found in green vegetables like broccoli, cabbage, and kale because the leaves of the plant shield the florets from the sun as they grow?

Ingredients:

1 tablespoon cumin seeds

1 whole cauliflower, cut into florets

2 tablespoons ghee or butter

1 onion, peeled and quartered

2 tomatoes, thickly sliced

1 kg (2¼ lb) mixed vegetables such as pumpkin, sweet potato, rutabaga, or kohlrabi (a sweet cabbage–turnip vegetable) cut into large chunks

140 g (5 oz) thickened tomato paste

1 cup (250 ml) vegetable stock

Sea salt and freshly ground black pepper

¼ teaspoon ground nutmeg

- Preheat the oven to 180°C (350°F/Gas mark 4).

- Fill a large deep pan with water to the halfway point. Add the cumin and cauliflower florets, bring to a boil, then reduce to a simmer for 5–10 minutes, until just cooked (al dente) and remove.

- Melt the ghee or butter in a pan and fry the cauliflower in batches until lightly golden. Drain each batch on paper towels.

- Place the cauliflower, onion, sliced tomato, pumpkin, sweet potato, and rutabaga, or whatever else you are using, into a large baking dish.

- Combine the tomato paste with the vegetable stock, salt, pepper, and nutmeg and pour it over the cauliflower. Bake in the oven for 40–45 minutes until the liquid has reduced and the vegetables are soft. Serve.

BAMYA | OKRA, LAMB, AND TOMATO STEW

Serves: 4

Okra, which is also known as 'ladies' fingers,' is a thin, green vegetable pod containing small white seeds arranged in vertical rows. It has an unusual texture and is very sticky when cut, and so acts as a thickener when used in stews. I have difficulty finding this vegetable fresh, but it can be found in Middle Eastern or Asian grocers or at markets. Look for vegetables that have a firm feel and are a uniform green color without blemishes. Alternatively, you can buy it frozen (use without thawing). If you would like to make a vegetarian version of *bamya*, simply eliminate the meat or substitute it with fresh green beans, Lebanese eggplant cut into cubes, or sliced zucchini.

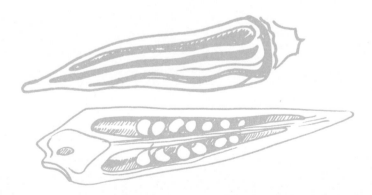

Ingredients:

2 tablespoons oil
1 onion, finely chopped
1–2 cloves garlic
500 g (1 lb) lamb tenderloin
1 teaspoon salt
¼ teaspoon freshly ground black pepper
½ teaspoon mixed spice
140 g (5 oz) thickened tomato paste
2 cups (500 ml) tomato sauce or passata
500 g (1 lb) young okra, frozen or fresh
Juice of half a lemon

• Heat the oil in a large heavy-based pan over a medium heat, then fry the onion and garlic for 2 minutes until lightly golden.
• Add the meat and cook until it is lightly browned and most of the liquid has evaporated. Add the salt, pepper, spice, tomato paste, and sauce and cook for a further 2 minutes.
• Ensure there is enough liquid to cover the meat, adding a little water if necessary. Bring to the boil over a high heat then reduce the heat and simmer gently, covered, for 45–60 minutes, or until the meat is cooked and very tender.
• While the meat is cooking, make sure the okra is free from bruising and cut off any stalk tops. Once the meat is cooked, add the okra and cook for a further 15 minutes. Add the lemon juice and stir to combine. Serve with rice.

BATATIS FI-L-FORN | EGYPTIAN ROAST BEEF AND POTATOES

Serves: 6

Potatoes are the third most important food crop in the world and are a staple for many people. In Egypt, however, it is rice that has a wider appeal. Growing up we had rice or bread or sometimes both as our staple, but I did love having potato for a change. This meal is a simple yet hearty dish that is wonderfully warming and filling in winter. My mum served it over rice for a double-carb loading. You could substitute potato with sweet potato if you are looking to lower the Glycaemic Index in this meal. It can also be nice to add other vegetables, such as thick slices of carrot and a garnish of peas.

Ingredients:

1 kg (2¼ lb) potatoes, peeled and thickly sliced

2 or 3 tomatoes, thickly sliced

1 onion, thickly sliced

1 tablespoon ghee or butter

1 kg (2¼ lb) beef (topside, shank, or round),
    cut into 10–12 pieces

140 g (5 oz) thickened tomato paste

1 teaspoon allspice

1 teaspoon salt

½ teaspoon freshly ground black pepper

2 cups (500 ml) tomato sauce or passata

• Preheat the oven to 180°C (350°F/Gas mark 4). Place the potatoes, tomatoes, and onion in a single layer in a large baking tray.

• Melt the ghee or butter in a pan over a high heat and fry the beef for several minutes until browned.

• Add the tomato paste, spice, and seasoning, and fry for around one minute. Then add the tomato sauce or passata and 2½ cups (625 ml) water. Bring to the boil, then pour the meat and sauce mix over the potatoes, tomatoes, and onion. The meat and potatoes should be at least half covered; if not, add more water.

• Bake in the oven for 2 hours. Check after 1½ hours that there is sufficient liquid—if not, add a little water. Turn the meat if it is browning too much. The dish is cooked when the liquid has reduced, the potatoes are well cooked, and the meat is tender.

ROAST VEGETABLE KIBBEH

Makes: 12–14

Since writing *The Taste of Egypt* I have met more and more vegetarian and vegan Egyptians and therefore I have tried to include more vegetarian versions of Egyptian recipes here. This is a dish that my mum made for us at home using ground beef and bulgur wheat, and that is similar in nature to the American meatloaf in many ways. My mother was from Cairo and this is a dish that she ate when growing up there. But my dad, who grew up in Minya (south of Cairo), had never eaten it until he met my mum. I actually really like the meatloaf version (the recipe is available in my book *The Taste of Egypt*) but here is a vegetarian version which I think is super tasty and a terrific alternative.

COOK'S TIP

The *kibbeh* can be frozen before the frying stage but thaw them out fully before cooking.

Ingredients:

2 tablespoons olive oil

1 kg (2¼ lb) sweet potatoes, washed, peeled,
    and cut into 2 cm cubes

450 g (1 lb) fine bulgur wheat, white or brown

1 large onion, finely grated and squeezed
    to remove excess juice

1 teaspoon ground cumin

1 teaspoon mixed spice

1 teaspoon ground coriander

½ bunch mixed fresh herbs (chives, lemon thyme,
    and/or parsley), finely chopped

Zest and juice of 1 lemon

Salt and freshly ground black pepper

2 tablespoons plain flour

Rice bran oil or vegetable oil, for frying

Filling:

400 g (14 oz) butternut squash, peeled and cut into 2 cm cubes
400 g (14 oz) sweet potatoes, peeled and cut into 2 cm cubes
100 g (3½ oz) carrots, washed and cut into 2 cm slices
1 large onion, peeled and finely chopped
½ bunch or 1 large handful of spinach leaves, washed
    and roughly chopped
1 teaspoon Lebanese mixed spice *(baharat)*,
    or ground coriander
1 teaspoon ground cumin
2 tablespoons pine nuts
100 g (3½ oz) canned chickpeas, drained
1 tablespoon sumac (optional)
Salt and freshly ground black pepper

• Preheat oven to 180°C (350°F/Gas mark 4).
• Drizzle olive oil on two baking trays. Place the sweet potato onto one of the baking trays. Season with salt and drizzle with a little more oil.
• On the second baking tray scatter the filling vegetables (squash, sweet potato, and carrot), drizzling with a little more oil and seasoning with salt. Roast both trays, uncovered, for 30 minutes or until the vegetables are tender, then remove from the oven and set aside to cool.

• Place the sweet potato cubes into a large mixing bowl. Add the bulgur and knead together to soften the wheat. Add a little boiling water if the mixture is too dry. Next add the grated onion, cumin, mixed spice, ground coriander, herbs, lemon zest and juice, and season with salt and pepper. Sprinkle the flour a little at a time while combining the ingredients together until it is a firm dough consistency. Cover with plastic wrap and refrigerate.

• To make the filling, heat the oil in a large frying pan over a medium heat and sauté the onion until translucent. Add the spinach leaves and cook until wilted. Stir in the mixed spice or coriander, cumin, and pine nuts. Add the roasted squash, sweet potato, and carrot, along with the chickpeas and sumac, if using. Season with salt and pepper then remove from the heat and set aside to cool.

• To assemble the *kibbeh,* have a small bowl of water handy to dip your fingers in from time to time whilst shaping the torpedoes. Take a small amount of the mixture and roll into a small ball about the size of an egg. Using your thumb, gently create a small cavity by rotating and pressing the mixture until it is approximately 1 cm thick. Stuff the cavity with some of the filling, then close the opening by shaping into a peak. Mould into a torpedo shape turning it around in the palm of your hands. Place on a tray lined with parchment paper and refrigerate for at least 30 minutes before frying.

• To cook the *kibbeh,* heat the oil in a deep-fat fryer or large pot to 180°C. Fry the *kibbeh* a few at a time, being careful not to overcrowd the pot, until they are a light golden brown color. Drain on paper towels and serve.

MESA'AA | EGYPTIAN MOUSSAKA

Serves: 6

This is one dish that particularly reminds me of my mother and of home. It was a dish I loved in summer when my mother would slice the eggplant and salt it, then leave it out in the sun for several hours in a colander to drain out the bitter liquid. She would then fry it in butter and layer it with ground beef before baking. I loved to eat this with rice and vermicelli (page 76).

When I left to go to university, I would make the two-hour commute home every weekend, and so often this delicious dish was waiting for me, made with love.

Ingredients:

1 kg (2¼ lb) eggplant

2 tablespoons salt

1 tablespoon vegetable oil

1 large onion, finely chopped

750 g (1½ lb) ground beef

400 g (14 oz) can chopped tomatoes

1 cup (250 ml) tomato sauce or passata

140 g (5 oz) thickened tomato paste

1 tablespoon thyme, finely chopped

1 tablespoon oregano, finely chopped

1 tablespoon basil, finely chopped

1 teaspoon mixed spice

Sea salt and freshly ground black pepper

30 g (1 oz) breadcrumbs

Vegetable oil, for frying

• Cut the eggplant into 1 cm (½ in) slices. Place the slices in a colander and salt liberally, tossing them to coat. Cover with a plate and weigh down with a can or jar. Place the colander in the sink (or outside as my mum used to do) for at least 30 minutes so that the bitter liquid can be drawn out.

• Rinse the excess salt from the eggplant slices, then dry them on paper towels and brush with oil. Fry in batches over a medium heat for 5 minutes each side until golden. As each batch cooks, remove to a plate lined with paper towels.

• Heat 1 tablespoon of oil in a large pan over a medium heat. Add the onion and fry until translucent. Add the beef and cook for around 15 minutes, until it is browned and almost all the liquid has evaporated.

•Add the tomatoes, tomato sauce or passata, and tomato paste, along with the herbs and spice, and cook for 2 minutes.

• Add 2 cups (500 ml) water, bring it to the boil, then reduce the heat and simmer uncovered until the meat is cooked and the liquid has almost completely evaporated. Season with salt and pepper.

• Heat the oven to 180°C (350°F/Gas mark 4). Grease a 20 by 15 cm (8 by 6 in) tray with oil and sprinkle the bread-crumbs over. Tap the tray to spread the crumbs in a thin layer and remove any excess.

• Layer half the eggplant over the base, then cover with half the cooked beef. Repeat with another layer of eggplant and the remainder of the meat. Bake, uncovered, for 40–45 minutes or until golden brown on top.

MAHSHI WARA' 'ENAB | STUFFED VINE LEAVES

Serves: 2

These stuffed vine leaves are always served on special occasions in our house. The time and effort required to make this dish is well worth it—my dad often says that this is the best food in the world! *Mahshi wara' 'enab* is famous throughout the Middle East, Lebanon, Syria, Jordan, Palestine, Egypt, and Iraq, but also well known in Greece and the Mediterranean. The mint seasoning makes the dish classically Lebanese, and in Greece these are served cold. In Egypt, unlike some other countries, it is eaten hot and as part of the main meal, rather than as an appetizer. The Egyptian version is also very small, comparatively speaking, and usually uses *khaltat wara' 'enab* as a stuffing, a mixture made from ground beef, rice, onions, and parsley. Fresh vine leaves are the best form to use if possible—if you have access to a grape vine, select leaves that are large but a lighter green than the older ones. I pick mine as and when I need them so they are as fresh as possible, but if you are not using them immediately you can freeze the leaves and use them later (simply thaw them out well and blanch them in boiling water as you would for freshly picked leaves). Vine leaves can also be bought canned, soaked in brine, from some supermarkets and delicatessens. Drain these and rinse before using.

Ingredients:

250 g (9 oz) ground beef
1 onion, finely chopped
½ cup flat-leaf parsley, finely chopped
100 g (3½ oz) white rice
½ teaspoon mace or mixed spice
Salt and freshly ground black pepper, to taste
250 g (9 oz) fresh vine leaves, plus extra for pan lining, or
200 g (7 oz) canned leaves
1–2 cups (250–500 ml) chicken or beef stock
3 tablespoons lemon juice
1 tablespoon olive oil

Mint yogurt sauce:

125 g (4½ oz) Greek-style yogurt
Handful fresh mint, very finely chopped
1 clove garlic, crushed
Juice of half a lemon
Pinch of salt

• Combine the ingredients for the mint yogurt sauce and set aside.

• In a bowl, combine the meat, onion, parsley, rice, mace or mixed spice, salt, and pepper.

• If you are using fresh vine leaves, bring plenty of water to the boil in a large pan and blanch in batches until they change from bright green to a khaki color. Set aside. If you are using canned vine leaves, soak them in water and drain 2 or 3 times to remove excess salt.

• Carefully separate all the vine leaves. Place each leaf shiny-side down, with its stem toward you. Put 1 teaspoon of the stuffing near the bottom of the leaf or stem, then fold the leaf: start by folding from the bottom up, then fold in the two sides to cover the filling, and complete by rolling tightly toward the tip of the leaf. Repeat the process until you have used all the stuffing.

COOK'S TIP

Place 3 or 4 lamb chops in the bottom of the pot and carefully layer the *mahshi* on top. These add flavor and taste delicious when cooked. Serve them alongside the *mahshi* or remove the chops and have these in a separate meal.

• If you are using fresh leaves, line a pan with a few of them to stop the stuffed leaves from sticking. These leaves will not be eaten, so older leaves are fine. Place the vine rolls in the pan (folded-edge down) and tightly packed together. Cover with several of the remaining vine leaves. (When my mother was cooking this, she would wrap any leftover stuffing in foil and place it on top to cook.) Cover the rolls completely with stock and add the lemon juice and oil. Cook for 25–30 minutes or until the rice and the leaves are tender and the liquid has evaporated. Serve with the mint yogurt sauce.

MAHSHI | MIXED STUFFED VEGETABLES IN TOMATO SAUCE

Serves: 4

Mahshi is a term used to refer to anything stuffed. In Egyptian cooking, vegetables are also often stuffed, not just cabbage leaves and vine leaves. The stuffing for this recipe can be used with zucchini, Lebanese eggplant, and bell peppers. A vegetable corer (known as a *ma'wara* in Arabic) is a popular tool that is used in the Middle East, and is as common as a vegetable peeler in the West. It is used to prepare vegetables such as zucchini and eggplant for stuffing and can be found in various kitchen stores or retailers. It is a long tool with a serrated edge on one side and a smooth edge on the other. There are two versions: one has a pointed end, which is good for piercing the vegetable flesh, and the other has a rounded end. They make the job of coring vegetables so much easier so I highly recommend using one.

Ingredients:

1½–2 kg (3–4½ lb) mixed vegetables, such as zucchini, eggplant, and bell peppers

3 cups (750 ml) tomato sauce or passata

4 cups (1 liter) beef stock

Stuffing:

500 g (1 lb) ground beef

1 teaspoon mixed spice

2 teaspoons oil, ghee, or melted butter (optional)

300 g (10½ oz) white short-grain rice

½ cup (125 ml) tomato sauce or passata

½ teaspoon allspice

1½ teaspoons sea salt

½ teaspoon freshly ground black pepper

2 medium onions, finely chopped or minced

1 bunch flat-leaf parsley, finely chopped

• Combine all the stuffing ingredients together in a bowl and mix well.

• Halve the eggplant and zucchini and use a vegetable corer to remove and discard the flesh, leaving a 1 cm (½ in) border. Do not puncture the ends. Cut the tops off the bell peppers and scoop out the insides.

• Stuff the vegetables with the meat mixture, making sure it is firmly packed, but be careful not to push the stuffing through the vegetable ends. Pack the vegetables into a large pan with the open ends facing upward.

• Pour the tomato sauce and stock over the vegetables, then add warm water to the pan until it comes up to the height of the vegetables. Bring to the boil over a high heat, then reduce to a medium heat and cook for 75–90 minutes or until the vegetables are tender and the rice is well cooked. Add boiling water to the pan during cooking if needed.

• Arrange the stuffed vegetables on a platter and serve hot.

COOK'S TIP

If you are left with any extra mince after stuffing the vegetables, wrap it in foil and place it on top of the vegetables during the last 10–15 minutes of cooking.

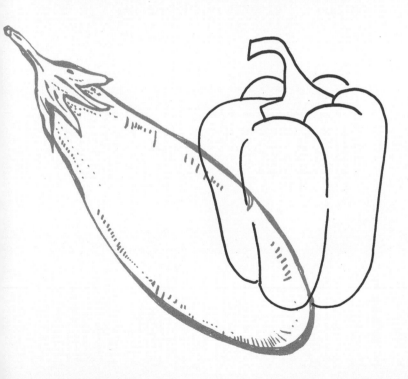

MAHSHI KROMB |
CABBAGE ROLLS WITH DILL

Serves: 6

Cabbage rolls may not sound very enticing, but these truly taste delicious. The cabbage leaves are parboiled with cumin and dill seeds which softens the leaves and makes them much easier to work with, while also infusing the leaves with flavor. These are then stuffed before being slowly cooked to perfection in a tomato-based sauce.

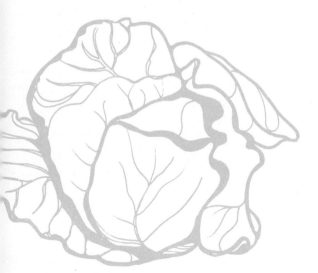

Ingredients:

1 whole cabbage
½ tablespoon dill seeds
½ tablespoon cumin seeds
1 tablespoon salt
3 cups (750 ml) tomato sauce or passata
4 cups (1 liter) salt-reduced beef stock

Stuffing:

1 teaspoon mixed spice
½ teaspoon allspice
1½ teaspoons salt
½ teaspoon ground black pepper
300 g (10½ oz) white short-grain rice
2 medium onions, finely chopped or minced
1 bunch flat-leaf parsley, finely chopped
500 g (1 lb) ground beef
1 teaspoon chopped dill

• Combine all the stuffing ingredients together in a bowl and mix well.

• Remove the outer leaves of the cabbage and cut out any hard core from each leaf. Keep these outer leaves for use later.

• Now separate the rest of the leaves from the cabbage. Fill a large pot with water and bring to the boil over a high heat. Add the dill, cumin seeds, and salt.

• Add the cabbage leaves to the water in batches—as many as your pan will allow. Cook until the leaves soften (about 5 minutes), then remove them from the water and set aside until all the leaves have been cooked.

• To fill, lay a leaf on a chopping board and spread it out fully. Place a line of stuffing at the center, leaving a 1 cm (½ in) border. Fold in the bottom end over the meat, tuck in the sides, and then roll to cover the stuffing. Cut off any excess. Repeat the process until all of the stuffing or leaves have been used.

• Layer the base of a pan with the reserved outer cabbage leaves. Place each of the cabbage rolls on top with the folded edge down, arranging them side by side in a layer. Build up the layers as necessary. When completed, put any leftover meat in foil and place on top of the cabbage rolls.

• Add the tomato sauce or passata then the beef stock, using as much as necessary to cover the rolls. (If they are still not covered, add water as required.) Place the pan over a high heat and bring to a boil, then reduce the heat and simmer for 50–60 minutes or until the meat and rice are cooked. Serve.

UL'AS | TARO WITH BEEF AND TOMATO

Serves: 6

Taro, or colocasia, is known as *ul'as* in Egypt. It is a root vegetable with twice the amount of fiber of a potato and is slightly sweeter when cooked. The hairy skin of the tuber is always removed before cooking as it can cause irritation, itching, and stomach upset. In Egypt there are two popular ways to cook *ul'as*. My mum always cooked it in chicken stock with fresh coriander and swiss chard. This is my version of the other, made with ground meat and tomato.

Ingredients:

2 tablespoons vegetable or rice bran oil

1 onion, finely chopped

1 kg (2¼ lb) ground beef

2 tomatoes, diced

140 g (5 oz) thickened tomato paste

2 cups (500 ml) tomato sauce or passata

1 teaspoon allspice

1 teaspoon mixed spice or Lebanese *baharat*

1 teaspoon salt

½ teaspoon freshly ground black pepper

4 cups (1 liter) beef stock or water

1 kg (2¼ lb) taro, peeled and thickly sliced

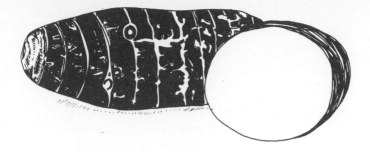

• Heat 1 tablespoon of oil in a large pan over a medium heat. Add the onion and fry until translucent. Add the beef and cook for around 15 minutes, until it is browned and almost all the liquid has evaporated. Break up any lumps as the meat is cooking.

• Add the tomatoes, tomato paste, and tomato sauce or passata, along with the allspice, mixed spice, salt, and pepper and cook for 2 minutes.

• Add 2 cups (500 ml) of the stock, bring to the boil, then reduce the heat and simmer uncovered until the meat is cooked and the liquid has almost completely evaporated. Season with salt and pepper.

• Heat the oven to 180°C (350°F/Gas mark 4). Grease a 20 by 15 cm (8 by 6 in) tray with 1 tablespoon oil.

• Layer half the taro over the base, then cover with half the cooked meat. Repeat with another layer of taro and the remainder of the meat. Carefully pour over the remaining 2 cups of stock and bake, uncovered, for 45–60 minutes until the liquid has evaporated and the taro is soft. Serve with bread or rice with vermicelli (page 76).

ROZ BI-L-SHA'RIYA | RICE WITH VERMICELLI

Serves: 4-6

This must be the most versatile way to cook rice. It can be served with almost anything and tastes great just on its own. I am always pleasantly surprised by the response I get from people when I make this for them. It is one of the staple recipes that I use during my cooking demonstrations on cruise ships as it is always popular and a simple dish that people can take away with them and try at home. If you would prefer to use brown rice instead of white, use an extra cup of liquid (250 ml) as brown rice is more fibrous and requires more liquid and longer cooking time.

Ingredients:

1 tablespoon ghee or butter
1 small handful crushed, dried vermicelli noodles
400 g (14 oz) jasmine or basmati rice
3 cups (750 ml) chicken stock
Sea salt

• Heat the ghee or butter in a pan over a medium heat and fry the vermicelli noodles for a few minutes, until lightly browned.

• Add the rice and stir continuously for 3–4 minutes until the rice grains are coated in butter and translucent. Some rice will turn opaque or white, which is fine, but do not allow any grains to burn. Add the chicken stock, and season with salt to taste.

• Bring to the boil over a high heat, stirring occasionally. Reduce the heat, cover, and simmer for 20 minutes. Do not stir the rice once it is simmering. Remove from heat, stir through, and serve.

ROZ AHMAR |
SALMON-COLORED RICE

Serves: 6

When I was growing up, my mum would make this rice to accompany grilled or fried fish. It has a lightly fragrant aroma from the sautéed onion and takes on a beautiful salmon-pink hue from the tomato, hence the name. I prefer to use basmati rice as it cooks well and is slightly better nutritionally than other white grains of rice. While ghee or butter is used for a fuller flavor when making rice with vermicelli (page 76), this rice is made with oil. My mum always used olive oil but I prefer to use rice bran oil here because it does not compete with the tomato and onion flavor.

Ingredients:

1 tablespoon rice bran oil
1 small onion, finely chopped
300 g (10½ oz) white basmati rice
3 tablespoons thickened tomato paste
2¼ cups (560 ml) water
Pinch of salt

• Heat the oil in a pan over a medium heat, add the onion, and fry until golden brown. Add the rice and stir for 2 minutes, then add the tomato paste and cook for a further minute.
• Pour in the water and taste for seasoning, adding salt as required. Stir and bring to the boil. Reduce the heat, stir, then cover and simmer for 20–25 minutes, stirring once toward the end of cooking.
• Remove from heat and serve.

MEAT, POULTRY, AND FISH

LAHMA BI-L-SHORBA | BRAISED BEEF CUBES

Serves: 4

This dish is simply slow-cooked meat but it is, despite its simplicity, really tasty. For those on a budget or using tough cuts of meat, this is perfect. Cuts like beef sirloin need to cook slowly and for longer than if you are using something like beef chuck. A pressure cooker or slow cooker are best to use. The pressure cooker will cut down the cooking time considerably but still results in lovely, tender meat. If you are using a slow cooker, use the lowest time setting for beef cut into small cubes. If you are leaving it in for longer then use large chunks of beef and check it occasionally to ensure it has not completely dried out. You could also use this method for other types of meat such as goat or rabbit, which can be tough when not slow cooked. Any leftovers can be used in a meat pie made with pastry or a cottage pie made with potato.

COOK'S TIP

Check the dish 15 minutes before the end of the cooking time; if there is too much liquid, add a little cornstarch mixed with cold water to thicken the sauce.

Ingredients:

1 tablespoon butter

3–4 cloves garlic, crushed

1 kg (2¼ lb) beef cut into 2 cm (¾ in) cubes

1 bay leaf

Sea salt and freshly ground black pepper

• In a large heavy-based pan or pressure cooker, melt the butter and fry the garlic over a medium heat for 2 minutes until golden in color. Do not allow it to brown.

• Add the beef and cook over a high heat until well browned. Do not worry if the base of the pan browns as this will add color and flavor to the liquid. Add the bay leaf and salt and pepper to taste. Cook for a further 2 minutes.

• Add enough water to cover the meat, then cover and cook on a low heat for 60 minutes (15–20 minutes if using a pressure cooker) until the meat is tender and cooked through.

KOBEBA |
BULGUR AND MEAT LOAF

Serves: 4–6

When I visit Egypt, I love to order *kobeba*. It is a delicious little egg-shaped parcel made with bulgur wheat and ground beef, and a spiced-meat stuffing, then deep fried.

In Lebanon it is known as *kibbeh* and eaten as part of a mezze. But at home, when my mum made this, we had it as a main meal served with a garden salad or tabouli. I have given the baked tray version here, which is the one I had growing up, but to make the individual appetizers take ¼ of a cup of the bulgur mix, flatten it, then use your palm to form a cup shape. Fill with the meat stuffing, then carefully close over the filling. Repeat to use up the mixture and keep in the fridge until ready to deep fry them. I prefer to serve these hot.

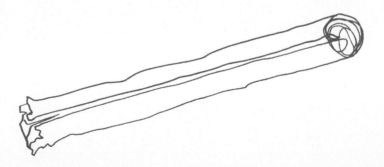

Ingredients:

500 g (1 lb) fine brown bulgur wheat

2–3 large onions, cut into quarters

500 g (1 lb) lean ground beef

2 teaspoons salt

½ –1 teaspoon freshly ground black pepper

1½ teaspoons mace or nutmeg

2 teaspoons cinnamon

Spiced meat filling:

2 tablespoons butter

1 large onion, finely chopped

500 g (1 lb) lean ground beef

1½ teaspoons cinnamon or mixed spice

1 teaspoon nutmeg, mace, or allspice

Sea salt and freshly ground black pepper

2 tablespoons pine nuts (optional)

100 g butter, softened

• Boil some water in a kettle. Place the bulgur wheat in a large bowl and cover it with the boiled water. Leave for 1–2 hours or until the water has been absorbed—the wheat should be soft and have doubled in volume. Remove any excess water by straining with a sieve and place the wheat into a large bowl.

• Next make the spiced meat filling. In a large pan, melt the butter and fry the onion for 2 minutes until golden. Add the meat and brown over a medium heat. Add the spices and season to taste. Add 1 to 2 cups (250–500 ml) of water to cover the meat. Bring to the boil on a high heat, then simmer until all the liquid has evaporated.

• Add the pine nuts, if using, and cook for a further 2 minutes.

• While the spiced mixture is simmering, blend the cooked bulgur, onion quarters, and ground beef in a food processor to a fine paste. Put the mixture into a bowl and add the salt, pepper, mace or nutmeg, and cinnamon. Set aside.

• Preheat the oven to 180°C (350°F/Gas mark 4). Grease a 30 by 25 cm (12 by 10 in) baking dish. Place half the bulgur and beef mixture into the dish and flatten using the palm of your hand. Then spread the spiced meat filling over the top. Use the remaining bulgur and beef mixture to cover the spiced meat. You may need to wet your hands to flatten the top layer.

• Cut the *kobeba* into squares. Place small dollops of butter on top, then place in the oven and bake for 30–40 minutes until the top is golden brown.

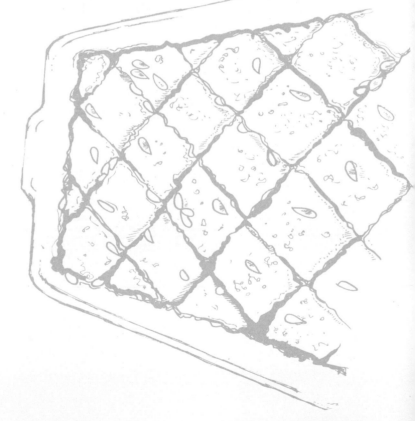

KOFTA BI-L-DEM'A | MEATBALLS IN SAUCE

Serves: 4

I loved having meatballs when growing up, and now I make these as part of a tasting plate to serve on board cruise ships when I present food and wine pairings. I always get lots of compliments as they are tasty but never dry. Try them as an appetizer at your next dinner party, serving them on a bed of sweet potato mash, like I do. Another great thing about this recipe is that you can make them ahead of time or make in double quantities and freeze (thaw out overnight in the fridge for best results). They can be served over rice or, for a more Italian feel, over pasta.

Ingredients:

500 g (1 lb) ground beef
1 medium onion, grated or finely chopped
1 clove garlic, crushed
¼ teaspoon sea salt
⅛ teaspoon freshly ground black pepper
½ teaspoon mixed spice or cinnamon
½ teaspoon ground cumin
1 tablespoon flat-leaf parsley, chopped
Ghee or vegetable oil, for frying
2 tablespoons rice flour

Tomato sauce:

1 tablespoon ghee or butter

1 medium onion, finely chopped

2 cloves garlic, crushed

1½ cups (375 ml) tomato paste
or passata

⅛ teaspoon freshly ground black pepper

¼ teaspoon salt

½ teaspoon mixed spice

½ teaspoon allspice

1 tablespoon basil, chopped

• Place all the ingredients for the meatballs in a bowl. Using your hands, combine together really well. Take a tablespoon of the mixture and roll into a ball about the size of a walnut. Place the meatball on a large plate. Repeat the process until all of the meat mixture has been used.

• Next make the tomato sauce. Melt the butter or ghee in a large pan over a medium heat and add the onion and garlic. Cook for 2 minutes, then add the tomato paste or passata and 1 cup (250 ml) of water. Add the pepper, salt, mixed spice, allspice, and basil, and bring to the boil. Reduce to a simmer while you cook the meatballs.

• Heat the ghee or vegetable oil in a frying pan and fry the meatballs—in batches if necessary—until browned all over. Alternatively, heat some oil in a deep-fat fryer and deep-fry the meatballs until well browned, then remove and drain on paper towels.

• Once all the meatballs are cooked, add to the sauce. The meatballs should be covered by the sauce; if not, add water as necessary.

• Cover and cook on a high heat for 10 minutes, then reduce to a medium heat for 15–20 minutes or until the meatballs are tender.

MACARONA FIL FORN | PASTA BAKE WITH BÉCHAMEL SAUCE

Serves: 6–8

Similar in design to a lasagne, this dish has ground beef sandwiched between pasta with a béchamel sauce on top. I often add vegetables to make a more complete meal, so feel free to improvise here if you want to. Vegetables such as carrot, celery, bell pepper, and mushrooms all work well and tend to go unnoticed by fussy eaters, so it's a good way of sneaking more vegetables into children's mouths. I also use up leftover roast vegetables in this dish too. Finely chop whatever you have and add it to the meat during cooking. It will add so much more flavor and body to the meat sauce.

Ingredients:

1 tablespoon ghee or butter
1 large onion, chopped
1 kg (2¼ lb) ground beef
1 teaspoon sea salt
¼ teaspoon freshly ground black pepper
1 teaspoon mace
240 g (8½ oz) thickened tomato paste
2¾ cups (690 ml) tomato sauce or passata
500 g (1 lb) rigatoni or penne pasta
60 g (2 oz) breadcrumbs

Béchamel sauce:

2 tablespoons butter
30 g (1 oz) plain flour
Sea salt and freshly ground black pepper
½ teaspoon mace or mixed spice
2½ cups (625 ml) milk
60 g (2 oz) strong cheese, grated
30 g (1 oz) parmesan cheese, grated

• Begin by making the meat sauce. Heat the ghee or butter in a pan over a medium heat and fry the onion until soft and golden brown. Add the ground beef, seasoning, and mace and continue to fry, breaking up any lumps. Continue to cook until the meat has browned and all the meat juices have evaporated.

• Add the tomato paste and cook for a further minute before adding the tomato sauce or passata and 2 cups (500 ml) of water. Reduce the heat and simmer, stirring occasionally, for 30–45 minutes or until the meat is cooked and there is only a thin film of liquid. Set aside.

• Preheat the oven to 180°C (350°F/Gas mark 4). Fill a large pot with water and bring to the boil. Add the pasta and cook as directed on the packaging. Strain, but do not rinse, as pasta should be sticky for this recipe.

• While the pasta is cooking, make the béchamel sauce. In a saucepan, melt the butter over a medium heat and add the flour. Cook for 2 minutes, stirring continuously, then add the seasoning and spices and cook for a further minute, still stirring. Add a little of the milk and stir to a smooth paste before adding more. Continue to add the milk in small amounts, stirring all the time to prevent any lumps forming. Bring to the boil, then reduce the heat and gently simmer until the sauce has thickened. Remove from the heat. Add the cheese and mix until smooth.

• Grease a large tray—around 30 by 26 cm (12 by 10 in)—and coat it with breadcrumbs. Reserve any excess. Using half the pasta, add a layer to the tray so that it covers the base.

• Add the meat on top of the pasta, spreading it evenly across the tray.

• Layer the remaining pasta evenly over the meat and cover with the béchamel sauce.

• Sprinkle the remaining breadcrumbs over the top. Bake for 45–50 minutes or until the top is golden brown.

KOFTA |
BARBECUED MINCE PARCELS

Serves: 4-6

These *kofta* are great for a summer barbeque but can also be made into the Middle Eastern answer to a hamburger—the good ol' kebab. Get some fresh pita bread, spread a layer of dip such as *tahina* (page 14), *hummus* (page 16), or *baba ghanoug* (page 18) on one side of the pita bread and add sliced onion, tomato, and lettuce with a few *kofta* on top. Wrap or roll and enjoy.

Ingredients:

500 g (1 lb) ground beef
500 g (1 lb) ground lamb
2 onions, finely minced
½ tablespoon salt
¼ tablespoon freshly ground black pepper
2 cloves garlic, crushed
1 teaspoon allspice
½ teaspoon mixed spice
1 bunch flat-leaf parsley, finely chopped
2 sheets caul fat (optional)

• Combine all ingredients, except for the caul fat, in a large bowl and use your hands to mix them together really well. Light the barbecue.

• If using caul fat, stretch out the fat 'net' on a board or clean surface. The fat often comes with sections of varying thicknesses and it is easiest to use the thinnest parts, so cut out any very thick sections of fat. Shape the meat into little sausages and place them at the edge of the caul fat, then roll the fat to cover the meat, making sure it overlaps a little. Cut it away from the caul fat sheet and repeat, making little sausages until the caul fat is used up.

• When the barbecue is ready, place the *kofta* on it, cut side of fat down, and use a gentle heat until cooked through. A charcoal or wood barbecue imparts a lovely smoky flavor to the *kofta*. Serve when cooked through.

COOK'S TIP

If you are not using caul fat, simply mix the ingredients together well, shape into sausages or wrap around a kebab stick, and cook over the barbeque. Turn frequently so they don't burn but make sure that they are cooked all the way through.

'AKKAWI | TWICE-COOKED OXTAIL

Serves: 4

This cut of meat is not as easy to find as it was in the past. As with most things, it comes in and out of fashion, but I really like it. The best place to find oxtail is in a large-produce market or a good butcher; if neither place stocks it, they may be willing to order it in for you. Twice-cooked oxtail is a simple dish with a deep flavor and the stock it produces is deliciously delicate. Do not be put off by the fat content as the fat is rendered off: simply reduce the stock by cooking, then cool and refrigerate overnight. This allows the fats to solidify for easy removal. The resulting stock is light but full of flavor, and it can be used to make other dishes such as *molokhiya* (page 38) or *fatta* (page 44).

> **COOK'S TIP**
> You can substitute 100 g (3½ oz) thickened tomato paste dissolved in 2 cups (500 ml) of water instead of the tomato sauce or passata.

Ingredients:

1 oxtail, cut into 7 or 8 pieces

1 onion, peeled with a cross cut into the top

Sea salt and freshly ground black pepper

1 bay leaf

4 potatoes, washed and cut into 2 cm (1 in) slices

2 large onions, peeled and thickly sliced

4 Roma tomatoes, thickly sliced or halved

2 cups (500 ml) tomato sauce or passata

• Place 6 cups (1½ liters) of water in a heavy-based pan and bring to the boil.

• Add the oxtail pieces along with the onion, salt, pepper, and bay leaf. Cover and cook gently on a low heat for 2 hours or until the meat is tender and separates from the bone. While the meat is cooking, remove any foam or impurities as they rise to the surface.

• When the meat is cooked, remove it from the stock and set aside.

• In a large baking tray, place the meat, potatoes, onions, and tomatoes so they are evenly distributed. Pour over the tomato sauce or passata.

• Bake in the oven at 180°C (350°F/Gas mark 4) for 40–60 minutes or until the vegetables are cooked and lightly browned. Serve.

TAGEN MOZA | LAMB TAGINE

Serves: 4

Lamb shanks remind me of winter. When the meat has been cooked well it is so incredibly tender that it just falls off the bone. In this recipe the shanks are slow cooked with potatoes and tomato, tucked inside a tagine in the oven. As with most dishes, the flavor of the meat will be enhanced if you use a homemade stock. I generally make the stock the day before I need it, which not only makes it easy to throw this dish together, but also means that you can leave it in the fridge overnight so that the fat will rise to the top and solidify, making it easy to remove. This makes the dish lighter and lower in saturated fat than it might be otherwise. Stock made from other dishes (such as *'akkawi*, page 96) can be frozen and used in making this dish. Simply thaw before using.

Ingredients:

4 lamb shanks
200 g (7 oz) sweet potatoes, peeled and cut into 2 cm (1 in) slices
1 large onion, sliced
4 cloves garlic, peeled
Sea salt and freshly ground black pepper

Stock:

4 lamb bones	2 bay leaves
Sea salt and freshly ground black pepper	1 large onion, peeled with a cross cut into the top
	½ bunch parsley, stalks intact

• Begin by making the stock. Place all the ingredients in a large pan or stock pot. Add just enough water to cover the bones and bring it to the boil over a high heat. Remove any impurities that rise to the surface, then reduce the heat and leave to simmer uncovered for 45–60 minutes. Add more water if the liquid reduces too much during cooking.

• After an hour, taste the stock to check the seasoning, remove the bones and then place back onto the heat to reduce further—aim for about 2 cups (500 ml) of liquid. Remove any fat from the surface, strain, and reserve the stock.

• Preheat the oven to 180°C (350°F/Gas mark 4).

• Place the lamb shanks, sweet potato, onion, and garlic in a large tagine or roasting dish, making sure they are well distributed.

• Season with salt and pepper and pour over 2 cups (500 ml) of stock. Place the tagine or roasting dish in the oven.

• If using a tagine, cover with the lid and bake for 2 hours; if using a roasting dish, leave it uncovered and bake for 60 minutes or until the meat is coming away from the bone and the sweet potato is cooked. After an hour of cooking, remove the tagine lid and cook for a further 30 minutes so that the meat develops a lovely color before serving.

FIRAKH FI-L-FORN | ROAST CHICKEN

Serves: 4

Some people choose not to eat chicken thighs, preferring the chicken breast pieces, but for me the thigh pieces are always my first preference. It takes a little longer to cook with the bones in, but they are far more tender and juicier than chicken breast, which can easily become overcooked and dry. These pieces are also easier to roast than a whole chicken, which needs cutting before serving and can be time consuming and fiddly for some. For entertaining you could substitute quail for the leg and thigh and cook using the same marinade given here. Just keep an eye on it during cooking as it is a small bird and will have a shorter cooking time.

COOK'S TIP

A tasty variation is to use lamb chops in place of the chicken.

Using 4 lamb chops, make a marinade by blending 2 peeled onions, 2 tomatoes, 1 clove garlic, 1 tablespoon mixed spice, and some salt and pepper in a food processor. Add a little water if necessary to help it form a paste-like consistency. Place the lamb chops in a large pan, add the marinade and ½ cup (125 ml) water. Cover and simmer for 2 hours on a low heat until tender. Serve over rice.

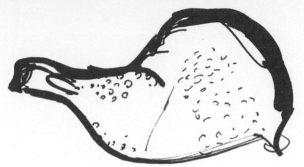

Ingredients:

4 chicken legs (thigh and drumstick together)

Marinade:

1 onion, minced
1 tomato, very finely diced
Juice of half a lemon
1 teaspoon sea salt flakes
½ teaspoon freshly ground black pepper
½ teaspoon mixed spice

• Preheat the oven to 180°C (350°F/Gas mark 4). Combine all the marinade ingredients in a bowl and mix well.
• Taking each chicken piece in turn, separate the skin from the flesh of the drumstick and thigh and rub the marinade under and over the skin.
• Place the chicken pieces in a baking dish and cover with any remaining marinade. Roast in the oven for 45—60 minutes until cooked. The skin should be crisp and the juices should run clear when the chicken is tested with a skewer at its thickest point. Serve with rice and salad, and perhaps some pickles and feta cheese. Yum!

FIRAKH MAHSHIYA FIREEK | FIREEK-STUFFED CHICKEN

Serves: 4–6

Fireek (also known as freekeh and farika) is a grain harvested from green, immature durum wheat. It can be found in delicatessens, Middle-Eastern grocery shops, and some supermarkets, and it makes a great stuffing. I love to use this for roast chicken—the grains are perfectly softened by chicken fat and perfumed oh-so-subtly by onion. Depending on the size of the chicken, you may have some stuffing left over. If so, push your fingers under the breast skin to make a pocket and then place any remaining stuffing under the skin. When cooking, you can keep the chicken especially moist by using an oven-safe roasting bag; just pierce the bag 4 or 5 times with a skewer to vent. Remove from the bag to serve but keep the juices as they make a terrific stock.

Ingredients:

1 tablespoon butter
1 small onion, finely chopped
110 g (4 oz) fireek
100 g (3½ oz) jasmine or long-grain rice
½ teaspoon sea salt flakes
¼ teaspoon freshly ground black pepper
1 large whole chicken

• Preheat the oven to 180°C (350°F/Gas mark 4). Melt the butter in a pan and fry the onion over a medium heat until lightly browned.

• Lower the heat, add the fireek and rice, and cook, stirring gently, for around 5 minutes (until the color changes slightly). Season with salt and pepper.

• Take the whole chicken and stuff the rice and fireek mixture into the breast cavity. Close the cavity by lacing 2 or 3 skewers over it or by sewing it shut with a heavy thread.

• Place the chicken breast-side-up on a greased rack inside a deep roasting dish. Cook on the center shelf of the oven for 25 minutes per 500 g (1 lb) plus 20 minutes. Check that it is cooked by pulling a leg away from the body and piercing between the leg and body—the juices should run clear and have no pink tinge. Stand for about 10 minutes before serving.

BANÉ / SCHNITZEL

Serves: 4

Schnitzels can be made using chicken, beef, veal, lamb or pork, although the Muslim countries of the Middle East do not use pork in any of their cuisine as it is a forbidden meat. I like to use lamb as it is more tender, but other meats will work well if you use a meat mallet to tenderize the meat first. The coating is very much the same—flour, eggs, and bread-crumbs. I use rice bran oil to fry as it is a neutral-tasting oil with a high smoke point. Make sure you have everything ready before making these and do not let the schnitzel sit in the coating for too long or they will not turn crispy when fried. Once coated fry immediately.

Ingredients:

4 veal or lamb steaks, thinly cut and tenderized
Salt and freshly ground black pepper
65 g (2¼ oz) plain flour combined with 1 teaspoon salt
2 large eggs, lightly beaten
70 g (2½ oz) plain breadcrumbs
Rice bran oil, for frying

• Place the steaks between two sheets of parchment paper and pound them with the smaller side of a meat tenderizer until just ¼ inch thick. Lightly season both sides with salt and freshly ground black pepper.

• Place the flour mixture, egg, and breadcrumbs in 3 separate shallow bowls. Dip the steaks first in the flour, then the egg, and then the breadcrumbs, coating both sides and all edges at each stage. Be careful not to press the breadcrumbs into the meat. Gently shake off excess crumbs.

• Half fill a large frying pan with oil and heat until it is hot—about 150°C (300°F).

• Fry the schnitzel for about 2–3 minutes on each side or until a deep golden brown.

Transfer to a plate lined with paper towels as soon as each is cooked, then serve immediately.

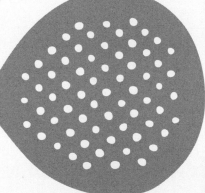

SAMAK MA'LI | FRIED FISH

Serves: 4

In recent years there has been more information regarding the health benefits of reducing red meat and consuming more sustainably sourced fish. While grilled fish simply seasoned with salt and pepper is delicious, sometimes it is nice to have fish that is bursting with flavor. You can experiment with different types of fish when cooking with this marinade, and for those that don't like the very 'fishy' smell or taste of fish this marinade is perfect.

COOK'S TIP

You can use the same marinade to cook a fish on the grill or barbecue. Just omit the flour and drizzle the fish with a little oil before cooking.

Ingredients:

4 firm white-fleshed fish, whole or fillets, such as Nile perch
Plain flour, for dipping
Vegetable or rice bran oil, for frying

Marinade:

2 cloves garlic, crushed
1 teaspoon ground cumin
Juice of 1 lemon
Sea salt and freshly ground black pepper

• First make the marinade by combining the garlic, cumin, lemon juice, and salt and pepper.
• Wash the fish, dry it with paper towels, then rub the marinade in and around the whole fish so it is well-coated. Refrigerate until ready to use.
• Put a little flour on a board and dip the fish into it, coating all sides before shaking off any excess.
• Place a frying pan over a medium-high heat, add the oil, then add the fish, once the oil is hot. Fry for 3–4 minutes on each side. Remove, drain on paper towels, and serve immediately.

SAMAK FI-L-FORN BI-L-FIREEK | BAKED FISH WITH FIREEK

Serves: 4

This dish is not something that you will find at a food court or even at a restaurant so if you're after something a little bit special, this is definitely worth the effort. Don't be intimidated by cooking a large whole fish—it is actually quite straightforward.

There are a few things to look out for when selecting fresh fish:

1. Look at the eyes to see how clear and plump they are (fish that are no longer very fresh have cloudy eyes that are dry and eventually collapse).
2. Check the gills: they should look wet and be a lively red/orange/brown color, not dried or dark brown.
3. A whole fish will smell like a fish, of course, but it should smell like a fish that's been recently plucked from marine or fresh waters. If it is starting to smell unpleasant, steer clear.
4. Lastly, a gentle press of the fish's flesh will see it spring back if it is fresh. If a dent remains in the flesh, it is past its prime.

Ask your fishmonger to scale and gut the fish for you. When you get home, give the fish a soak in salt water, then pat it dry with paper towels and season it inside and out with a little salt and pepper.

Ingredients:

1 large whole firm white-fleshed fish, such as trout, bream, or snapper

1 portion fish marinade (page 106)

225 g (8 oz) fireek

2 tablespoons thickened tomato paste

1 teaspoon ground cumin

Sea salt and freshly ground black pepper

Flour, for coating

Vegetable oil, for frying

1 tablespoon olive oil

1 tablespoon fresh parsley, chopped

Lemon wedges, to serve

• Preheat the oven to 180°C (350°F/Gas mark 4). Prepare and marinate the fish as for fried fish (page 106).

• Wash and drain the fireek, and place it in a large baking dish.

• Combine the tomato paste with 1 cup (250 ml) of water. Add the ground cumin and season with salt and pepper. Pour the mixture over the fireek.

• Put a little flour on a board and dip the fish into it, coating all sides before shaking off any excess. Place a frying pan over a medium-high heat, add the oil, then add the fish once the oil is hot. Fry for 3–4 minutes on each side.

• Put the fried fish on top of the fireek, drizzle olive oil on top, then put the dish in the oven for 15–20 minutes until cooked and fluffy. Remove from the oven, sprinkle with chopped parsley, and serve with lemon wedges.

SWEET DELIGHTS

BASBOUSA BI-L-LOZ | SEMOLINA CAKE WITH ALMONDS

Makes: 24

Basbousa is a syrup-drenched semolina cake. It is a traditional Egyptian sweet that has many variations: with or without nuts, made with butter, yogurt, or milk, flavored with vanilla, rose water, or orange-blossom water. I even made a dairy free version for my young daughter which tasted so good I put it in my book *The Taste of Egypt*. However, for me, vanilla is 100% my favorite flavor. I have used less syrup in this recipe so that it is a slightly firmer cake.

Ingredients:

250 g (9 oz) semolina
225 g (8 oz) sugar
250 g (9 oz) unsalted butter, plus extra for greasing
1 cup (250 ml) milk
140 g (5 oz) self-rising flour
15 raw almonds, skins removed and halved

Syrup:

400 g (14 oz) sugar
1 cup (250 ml) water
Juice of half a lemon
3–4 drops vanilla extract or
    1–2 tablespoons rose/orange-blossom water

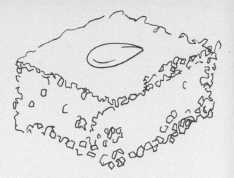

• Begin by making the syrup. Combine the sugar, water, and lemon juice in a small pan, bring to the boil, then turn down the heat and simmer for 10 minutes or until the syrup is thick enough to coat a spoon. Leave to cool. Once cooled, add the vanilla or flavored water and stir.

• Preheat the oven to 180°C (350°F/Gas mark 4). Lightly grease a 30 by 25 cm (12 by 10 in) cake tin with butter.

• Place the semolina and sugar in a large bowl and combine. Melt the butter, then add to the bowl along with the milk and flour, mixing well after each addition.

• Transfer the cake mixture to the baking tin. Mark out 24 squares and place the almond halves in the center of each square. Place in the oven and bake for 50–60 minutes or until golden brown.

• Remove the *basbousa* from the oven and carefully pour the cold syrup evenly over the hot cake. The temperature difference between the syrup and the cake results in greater absorption, so don't be tempted to leave both to get to room temperature. Serve when the cake has cooled.

BA'LAWA | BAKLAVA

Makes: 24 squares

This well-known sweet is popular all over the Mediterranean but has also become popular throughout much of the world. The crunchy nuts and pastry are a great combination with the sticky, sweet syrup.

The key to the success of this dish is to brush each sheet of pastry really well with melted ghee. This adds flavor but, more importantly, provides a crispness to the layers. Ghee is used here because the milk solids in butter can easily burn, which will ruin your baklava. Filo pastry sheets are very thin and can tear easily, and they also dry out quickly which causes them to break. To avoid this, place a slightly damp kitchen towel over the unused sheets of pastry as you work to prevent them from drying out. Traditionally baklava is made with chopped nuts, which give it a rich taste and add to the crispy, crunchy texture, but I enjoy the contrasting texture of sultanas or currants scattered throughout. You can add lots of these or just a few—or omit them entirely if you prefer.

Ingredients:

225 g (8 oz) pistachios, walnuts, or
    almonds, coarsely chopped
60 g (2 oz) sugar
1 teaspoon ground cinnamon
½ teaspoon ground cloves
1–2 tablespoons sultanas or currants (optional)
250 g (9 oz) ghee, plus extra for greasing
375 g (13 oz) filo pastry, at room temperature

Syrup:

400 g (14 oz) sugar
2 cups (500 ml) water
Juice of half a lemon
3–4 drops vanilla extract

• Begin by making the syrup. Combine the sugar, water, and lemon juice in a pan. Bring to the boil, then turn down the heat and simmer for 10 minutes until the syrup reduces and becomes thick enough to coat the back of a spoon. Add the vanilla and leave to cool.

• Preheat the oven to 180°C (350°F/Gas mark 4). In a bowl, combine the chopped nuts, sugar, cinnamon, cloves, and any sultanas or currants.

• Lightly grease the base and sides of a 30 by 25 cm (12 by 10 in) cake tin with ghee. Melt the remaining ghee.

• Take the filo sheets from their packaging and place them on a chopping board or plate, then cover the filo sheets with a damp kitchen towel. Remove a single sheet of filo pastry at a time. Taking the first sheet, fold it in half and place it in the tray. Brush the top with melted ghee and fold in the edges to fit, if necessary. Repeat this process for half of the filo sheets, making sure you brush each sheet with ghee, and folding the sides where necessary to fit the tray.

• Sprinkle the nut mixture over the pastry in the tray and then continue to layer the pastry with the remaining sheets, following the same process as before. When you have used all the sheets, pour any remaining ghee over the top.

• Cut the layered pastry into 24 diamond or square shapes, making sure to cut right through to the base.

• Place in the center of the oven and bake for 20–25 minutes or until the baklava is puffed and lightly golden on top.

• Remove from the oven and pour the cooled syrup over the hot baklava. Leave to cool before cutting along the diagonals again to remove from the tray.

COOK'S TIP

This can be prepared one day and baked the next. Cover and store the layered pastry in the refrigerator overnight and bake shortly before you want to eat it. Baklava will also keep for several days after baking in an airtight container at room temperature. Do not store it in the refrigerator after baking or the sheets will go soggy.

KONAFA BI-L-MIKASSARAT | KONAFA WITH MIXED NUTS

Makes: 1 cake

My mum was an expert at making this sweet and would experiment with the pastry, making different shapes with it. This recipe is the easier and far less time-consuming cake style, but feel free to experiment with various shapes or patterns yourself. You can use just one kind of nut or a combination of two or three to suit your own taste. If it does not get eaten all at once, cover the *konafa* with plastic wrap and keep at room temperature; do not store in the refrigerator or, just like baklava, the pastry will go soggy. Traditionally the very thin batter is run through a sieve onto a hot plate to create the strands, but this is very fiddly to recreate at home. Thankfully the pastry can be found fairly easily in many supermarkets or Mediterranean grocers. If you can't find it fresh you may be able to find it frozen. Just thaw before using.

Ingredients:

225 g (8 oz) pistachios, walnuts, or almonds, coarsely chopped

3 tablespoons sugar

1 teaspoon ground cinnamon

½ teaspoon ground cloves

375g (13 oz) *konafa*

250 g (9 oz) unsalted butter or ghee

Syrup:

225 g (8 oz) sugar

1 cup (250 ml) water

Juice of half a lemon

3–4 drops vanilla extract

• Begin by making the syrup. Combine the sugar, water, and lemon juice in a pan. Bring to the boil, then reduce the heat and simmer for 10 minutes until the syrup reduces and becomes thick enough to coat the back of a spoon. Leave for 5 minutes to cool, then add a few drops of vanilla essence and stir.

• Preheat the oven to 180°C (350°F/Gas mark 4). Combine the nuts, sugar, and spices in a bowl.

• Pull apart the *konafa* strands in a bowl and pour melted butter over them. Mix thoroughly with your fingers to coat and separate the strands.

• Lightly grease a large, deep, round dish (diameter around 25 cm/10 in) and put half the pastry into it. Flatten the pastry with the palm of your hand. Spread the nut mixture evenly over it and cover with the remaining pastry. Flatten the top again.

• Put into the center of the oven and bake for 60–65 minutes or until golden in color. Remove the *konafa* from the oven and pour the cooled syrup over the top. Leave it to cool to room temperature, then cover with a plate and turn over to remove. Cut and serve.

COOK'S TIP

The *konafa* may be made into individual portions by separating the strands, placing some nut mixture at the end of each one, and rolling each stuffed strand into tight little logs. Place these on a tray cut-side down before baking for 20–25 minutes, and drizzle 1 or 2 tablespoons of syrup over each.

SHA'RIYA BI-L-LABAN | NOODLES WITH MILK

Serves: 4

Perfect as a dessert or a snack in winter, *sha'riya bi-l-laban* is similar to rice pudding but made with noodles. It is commonly eaten in upper Egypt and in rural villages, where they tend to use wheat dough to make long thin strands of noodles (which are dried before use) and which are then cooked with buffalo milk. I have never seen the noodles made and have not tried making them myself—I use dried wheat noodles that I find in the Asian or International food aisle of the supermarket. If you toast the noodles to a brown color before putting them in the milk they impart an almost nutty flavor to this dish, and I think it is well worth taking the time to do so. For an even more complex taste, use brown sugar which contains a hint of caramel flavor—so good!

Ingredients:

250 g (9 oz) dried wheat noodles
5 cups (1¼ liters) milk
115 g (4 oz) sugar, or as desired
60 g (2 oz) butter
1 teaspoon vanilla extract

- Preheat the oven to 200°C (400°F/Gas mark 6). Wrap the noodles in a clean kitchen towel and use a meat mallet or rolling pin to break them up.
- Place all the noodle pieces on an oven tray—even the little bits. Bake in the oven for 10–15 minutes, turning occasionally, until the noodles are mostly browned. It is better to have more of them brown than creamy colored, but don't overcook and burn them, and don't worry if some are not as browned as others.
- While the noodles are toasting, place the milk and sugar in a medium-sized pan and heat on a medium heat until hot but not boiling.
- Remove the noodles from the oven and add to the hot milk. Reduce the heat to a low simmer and cook for 15–20 minutes or until the noodles are soft, stirring occasionally and breaking up any lumps as they cook and soften. Keep an eye on the milk to make sure it doesn't boil over.
- When cooked, remove from the heat and stir in the butter and vanilla extract. Serve immediately with a little extra milk, if desired.

MIHALLABIYA | ALMOND CUSTARD

Serves: 4

This has a custard-like consistency and can be served hot in winter or thinned by adding more milk and served cold as a drink in summer. I make this dish regularly during my cooking demonstrations on board cruise ships. It always gets a great response during tastings by my audience, whom I welcome up on stage to add their preferred garnish, just like they would at home.

Ingredients:

2 tablespoons rice flour
2 tablespoons cornstarch
4 cups (1 liter) milk
115 g (4 oz) sugar, or as desired
3–4 drops vanilla essence
100 g (3½ oz) ground almonds
Chopped pistachios or blanched almonds, to decorate

• Combine the flour and cornstarch and mix with ¼ cup (60 ml) of the milk to make a smooth, thick paste.
• Add the sugar to the remaining milk, place in a pan, and bring just to the boil over a medium heat.
• Reduce the heat and add the flour paste gradually, stirring constantly so it does not boil or go lumpy. Cook for 10–15 minutes until there is a slight resistance and the mixture coats the back of the spoon.
• Add the vanilla essence and cook for a further 2 minutes. Remove from the heat and stir in the ground almonds.
• Cool a little before dividing into individual ramekins or glasses. Refrigerate for 3–4 hours and serve decorated with chopped almonds or pistachios, if desired.

ZALABYA |
SYRUP-DRENCHED DONUTS

Makes: approximately 50

Zalabya are golden donut balls of heavenly sweetness. They are made by deep-frying dough and then, as with so many Egyptian sweets, soaking them in thick sugar syrup. The donuts are very similar to the Greek *loukoumades*—which are soaked in a honey syrup. *Zalabya* are great for a large gathering where there will be plenty of people to enjoy them. They also have a wow factor that makes them fun for dinner parties. These do not keep well when stored and the best crunch is when they are freshly cooked, so serve these immediately.

Ingredients:

2 teaspoons dried yeast

1 teaspoon sugar

140 g (5 oz) plain flour, sifted

Corn oil, to deep fry

Syrup:

400 g (14 oz) sugar

2 cups (500 ml) water

Juice of half a lemon

4–5 drops vanilla extract

• Begin by making the syrup. Combine the sugar, water, and lemon juice in a pan and place over a medium heat to dissolve the sugar. Bring the syrup just to the boil and simmer for 10 minutes. Turn off the heat and leave to cool. Add the vanilla and stir well.

• Place the yeast, sugar, and 2 tablespoons of warm water in a cup. Stir then leave in a warm place for 10 minutes until bubbles form. (If there are no bubbles it means the yeast is dead and you will need to start again with fresh yeast.)

• Sift the flour into a large bowl, make a well in the center, and add the yeast. Add 1 cup (250 ml) warm water and mix together to form a smooth consistency. Cover the batter with a kitchen towel and leave to rise in a warm place for 2 hours or so, until it doubles in size. The time will depend on the temperature—the batter will need a warm, not hot, environment to rise.

• Heat the oil in a deep-fryer over a high heat. When the oil is just starting to smoke, drop a teaspoonful of the batter into the hot oil. It should immediately expand in size. Add several spoonfuls, so you are cooking a few *zalabya* at a time. When they have turned golden brown on one side, turn them over.

• When each batch is cooked, remove the donuts and place them directly into the syrup, turning them over to make sure they are fully coated. Leave for a few minutes then remove from the syrup and drain in a colander or sieve over a bowl. Repeat for each batch. Serve immediately.

COOK'S TIP

It is best to be very organized before beginning to fry the *zalabya*. Position the batter close to the oil so that you are not reaching over to get it. Place the syrup next to the oil on the other side so that you can easily remove the donuts with a long, slotted spoon or tongs and dunk them in the syrup. Next to the syrup, place a colander sitting over a bowl, with another slotted spoon or tongs, for draining the syrup from the donuts. When one batch of *zalabya* is sitting in syrup, add the next batch into the oil—only remove those sitting in the syrup just before the next batch is ready to come out of the oil.

ATAYEF |
CRUNCHY SYRUP PILLOWS

Makes: 30–35

Atayef comes from the work *qataf* which means 'to pick up.'
Atayef are ultra-delicious and are made in abundance during
Ramadan in Egypt, sold by street vendors as well as being
commonly made in households. Beautifully crunchy, these
nut-filled pillows are drenched in sugar syrup. In Lebanon
these may be made with a ricotta filling but I always eat
them filled with chopped nuts. Pistachios are often used and
have a great color but you could use whatever nuts you like,
including walnuts, almonds, or hazelnuts. In trying to perfect
this recipe I remembered how my mother and I once worked in
the kitchen for many hours trying to get the batter to the right
consistency. It was therefore not a regular feature in our household! My mum (who did not use recipes when she cooked)
made this dish so rarely that she when she did go to make
it, she had completely forgotten how. *Atayef* are best served
immediately after cooking, so only fry what you need. These
can, however, be prepared up to the frying stage and kept covered in the refrigerator for a few hours until required, or even
frozen. Remember to place parchment paper between layers
before freezing and completely thaw them out before frying.

Ingredients:

170 g (6 oz) crushed walnuts
1 tablespoon sugar
2 tablespoons sultanas (optional)
1 sachet (7 g) dried yeast
1 teaspoon sugar
225 g (8 oz) plain flour
Corn oil, for deep-frying

Syrup:

400 g (14 oz) sugar
2 cups (500 ml) water
Juice of half a lemon
1 teaspoon vanilla extract

COOK'S TIP

When bringing the flour, water, and yeast together do not be afraid to get your hands dirty. This recipe is easiest made using your fingertips, just as you would when making fresh pasta.

You can leave the pancakes flat and deep-fry them without stuffing. They taste great, especially when accompanied with double cream and fresh fruit such as strawberries or blueberries. I add a little sugar and a few drops of vanilla extract to the cream before serving.

• To make the stuffing, combine the crushed walnuts, sugar, and sultanas (if using) in a small bowl. Set aside.

• To make the syrup, combine the sugar, water, and lemon juice in a pan, bring to the boil over a medium heat, then lower the heat and cook for 8–10 minutes. The syrup should be a thin consistency. When cooked, remove from the heat and leave to cool. Once cooled, add the vanilla and stir. Set aside.

• While the syrup is cooking, make the batter. Place the yeast, sugar, and ¼ cup (60 ml) of warm water in a cup, stir, then leave in a warm place for 10 minutes until bubbles form. (If there are no bubbles the yeast is dead and you will need to start again with fresh yeast.)

• Sift the flour into a large bowl, make a well in the center, and add the yeast mixture. Add 1½ cups (375 ml) of warm water and mix together to a smooth consistency. Cover with a kitchen towel and leave to rise in a warm place for 1–2 hours until the batter doubles in size.

• Heat a non-stick frying pan on a medium heat without oil or butter. Mix the batter with a dessert spoon and then use the spoon to collect about half a spoonful and place it into the frying pan. Spread it thinly and evenly to a 10 cm (4 in) diameter—like a small, slightly thicker kind of crêpe. Cook on one side only and remove from the heat when the pancake has changed from white to yellow. Place on a clean dish and repeat until all the batter has been used.

• Place a teaspoon of the stuffing into the center of each pancake on the uncooked side. Fold over each one, pressing the edges firmly together, to form a half moon.

• Heat the oil in a deep-fat fryer over a high heat. Test for the correct temperature by placing a drop of batter in the oil—it should bubble immediately. Carefully place 2 or 3 *atayef* into the oil at a time, and fry until golden brown in color, turning as required.

• Remove each one from the oil as it is cooked and place directly into the cooled syrup, turning to coat. Remove from the syrup and leave to drain in a colander or sieve. When they are all cooked, serve immediately.

ROZ BI-L-LABAN | RICE PUDDING

Serves: 4

Rice pudding is a classic and very simple dessert that is so comforting during winter months. It takes me back to when I was a small child—what kid does not like sweetened milky rice! In Egypt it is not made by adding pre-cooked rice to milk but rather by cooking the rice in the milk. This method means that milk can burn and ruin the pudding and I have done this on more than one occasion in my time. To avoid this you must stir it constantly. My mother would make this when I was young then leave the bowls covered in the fridge and we would eat it for breakfast or as a snack. Gently reheat in the microwave with a little extra milk, until it reaches the desired consistency and serve with chopped nuts, sultanas, or cinnamon sugar.

Ingredients:

2 cups (500 ml) milk

2 cups (500 ml) coconut milk

170 g (6 oz) short-grain white rice

60 g (2 oz) white sugar, or as desired

40 g (1½ oz) butter

½ teaspoon almond essence or vanilla extract

Maple syrup, cinnamon, sultanas, or chopped almonds, to
   decorate before serving.

• Pour the milk and coconut milk into a heavy-based pan and
place over a medium heat. Bring just to the boil, then add
the rice and reduce the heat. Cook uncovered, at a simmer,
for 30–35 minutes, or until the rice is tender. Stir the rice
occasionally to prevent a skin from forming on the surface.
Add extra milk or water if all the liquid is absorbed before the
rice is cooked through.

• When cooked and creamy, add the sugar and stir well until
dissolved.

• Take the pudding off the heat and stir in the butter and
almond or vanilla flavoring. Transfer to serving bowls and
sprinkle with cinnamon, sultanas, or chopped almonds—or
all of these—if desired.

OMM 'ALI | EGYPTIAN BREAD-AND-BUTTER PUDDING

Serves: 4

When I was in Egypt for the *The Taste*—a Middle Eastern cooking show—I remember going to the food court at a shopping center on our day off. I was sitting with one of the competitors, who had his little son on his lap, eating *Omm 'Ali*. I never grew up eating this dessert but this little boy was enjoying it so much I went and bought some for myself.

This is a traditional Egyptian dessert akin to the Western bread-and-butter pudding, but without the eggs. If you have day old croissants this would be a great way to use them up, just rip them into pieces and place in an oven-proof bowl or ramekins. Alternatively, you can use 2 sheets of puff pastry (*mille feuille*) that has been baked in a medium oven until it has puffed up and is golden brown. *Omm 'Ali* can be prepared and left covered in the fridge for a few hours, making it great to prepare as a desert for a dinner party.

Ingredients:

2 sheets puff pastry (*mille feuille*)

30 g (1 oz) almonds, chopped

30 g (1 oz) pistachio nuts, chopped

40 g (1½ oz) sultanas

30 g (1 oz) desiccated coconut

4 cups (1 liter) full-cream milk

1 cup (250 ml) heavy cream

115 g (4 oz) sugar

Pinch or two of ground cinnamon

• Preheat the oven to 180°C (350°F/Gas mark 4).

• Place the sheets of puff pastry onto non-stick baking trays and bake for 8–10 minutes until puffed up and light golden brown. Remove from the oven.

• Place one sheet of pastry in a square baking dish and press down to break it up a little. Sprinkle over the chopped almonds and pistachio nuts, sultanas, and coconut. Cover with the remaining sheet of pastry and press down to break it up a little.

• In a saucepan, add the milk, cream, sugar, and ground cinnamon. Place over a medium heat and carefully warm up, stirring continually. Do not let it boil.

• Use a jug to pour the milk mixture over the pastry and place it in the oven for 15 minutes or until the liquid has been absorbed and the sheets are golden brown on top. Serve warm.

PETTIFORE | PETITS FOURS

Makes: 30–50

These are the best-looking cookies you can make, in my opinion, and very popular with kids. Buttery biscuits sand-wiched with strawberry jam, then dipped in chocolate and coated in nuts. Delicious! They are really fun to make with family or friends as you can all sit around and chat while they get assembled in a production line—just as my parents did when I was growing up.

Pettifore keep well in an airtight container and are so more-ish that I can never stop at just one. You can showcase them in their full glory by placing them under a covered glass display stand.

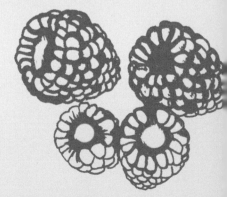

Ingredients:

225 g (8 oz) unsalted butter, plus extra for greasing
200 g (7 oz) caster sugar
1 egg
½ teaspoon vanilla essence
350–500 g (12–18 oz) self-rising flour
Strawberry or raspberry jam, for filling
250 g (9 oz) cooking chocolate, melted
Crushed peanuts or chocolate sprinkles,
   for coating (optional)

COOK'S TIP

To make chocolate cookies, take half the mixture
and place it into a clean bowl. Gently fold in 1 or 2
tablespoons of cocoa powder. To give the cookies a
marbled look, add only 1 tablespoon of cocoa powder
to the entire mixture and gently fold it through just a
few times, leaving it only partially mixed in.

- Preheat the oven to 160°C (325°F/Gas mark 3).
- Using an electric mixer, beat the butter and sugar together until light and fluffy, then add the egg and continue to beat until combined.
- Add the vanilla essence and then start adding the flour, a little at a time, scraping down the sides as you go, until the mixture is just coming together to form a ball. It should still be quite soft.

• Lightly grease a baking tray with butter. Roll the mixture into 30–40 walnut-sized balls and place them well apart on the tray. Dust your hands with flour and then flatten the balls with your fingers, to cookie thickness. You can also make lines, dots, or indentations with a fork to create different patterns.

• Bake for 12–15 minutes or until the cookies are lightly golden. Remove from the oven, leave for 2 minutes, then carefully take them off the tray using a metal spatula.

• Once cooled, divide the cookies into pairs of roughly even sizes. For each pair, spread jam on one cookie and then put the other cookie on top.

• To finish, dip a third or half of the paired cookies into melted chocolate and coat with crushed nuts or sprinkles. Serve or store in an airtight container.

KAHK | ICING SUGAR SHORTBREAD COOKIES

Makes: 20

As with all shortbread, these cookies have a high butter and sugar content, and so are quite heavy and sweet. I used to make them and take them to work sometimes, where they were all quickly gobbled up, and at home they are popular at celebrations such as Christmas and Easter. In Egypt these are an essential component of the Muslim *Eid el-Fitr*, the feast after Ramadan (the month in which Muslims fast from sunrise to sunset). The shortbread is so popular at that time it is a good indication of the arrival of Eid. *Kahk* probably originated in ancient Egypt around the peak of Egyptian power during the Eighteenth Dynasty (1550–1292 BCE). The inner walls of Kheime Ra's tomb in Thebes have pictures of this ancient Egyptian sweet adorning the walls. It was likely made using honey and flour, pressed into molds and decorated with the imprint of the sun before baking. *Kahk* fillings can vary; favorites include nuts—such as pistachios, walnuts, and almonds—or Turkish delight *(malban)*. *Kahk* with pitted, puréed dates *('agwa)* is more common in other parts of the Arab world, where it is known as *ma'mul*.

Ingredients:

250 g (9 oz) unsalted butter,
   softened, plus extra for greasing
45 g (1½ oz) icing sugar, plus extra to coat
1 egg yolk
¼ teaspoon vanilla extract
1 teaspoon baking powder
75 g (2½ oz) self-rising flour
140 g (5 oz) plain flour, plus extra
70 g (2½ oz) crushed walnuts or almonds

• Preheat the oven to 180°C (350°F/Gas mark 4). Lightly grease two oven trays and cover with baking or parchment paper.
• Using an electric mixer, beat the butter and icing sugar until light and fluffy. Add the egg yolk and vanilla extract and beat well to combine.
• Sift the baking powder and flours together. Gradually add this to the mixture, along with the nuts, and combine. The mixture is ready when it comes together as a ball of dough. Remove from the mixer and place on a floured board.

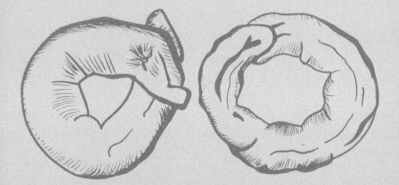

• Form the dough into little balls about the size of walnuts and flatten slightly with a fork. Alternatively, mould into thin sausages about 10 cm (4 in) long and 1 cm (½ in) wide, then bring the ends together to form a horseshoe shape. Place the dough shapes onto the baking trays, allowing room for spreading, and bake for approximately 10 minutes or until the cookies are slightly browned on the base.

• Remove from the oven and leave for a few minutes before sifting a little icing sugar over the top. Remove to a cooling rack to cool completely. When cooled, sift extra icing sugar on to them so they are well coated. Store in an airtight container out of the refrigerator, if there are any left!

INDEX